Adult Coloring Book
Mandala For Relaxation Volume 1

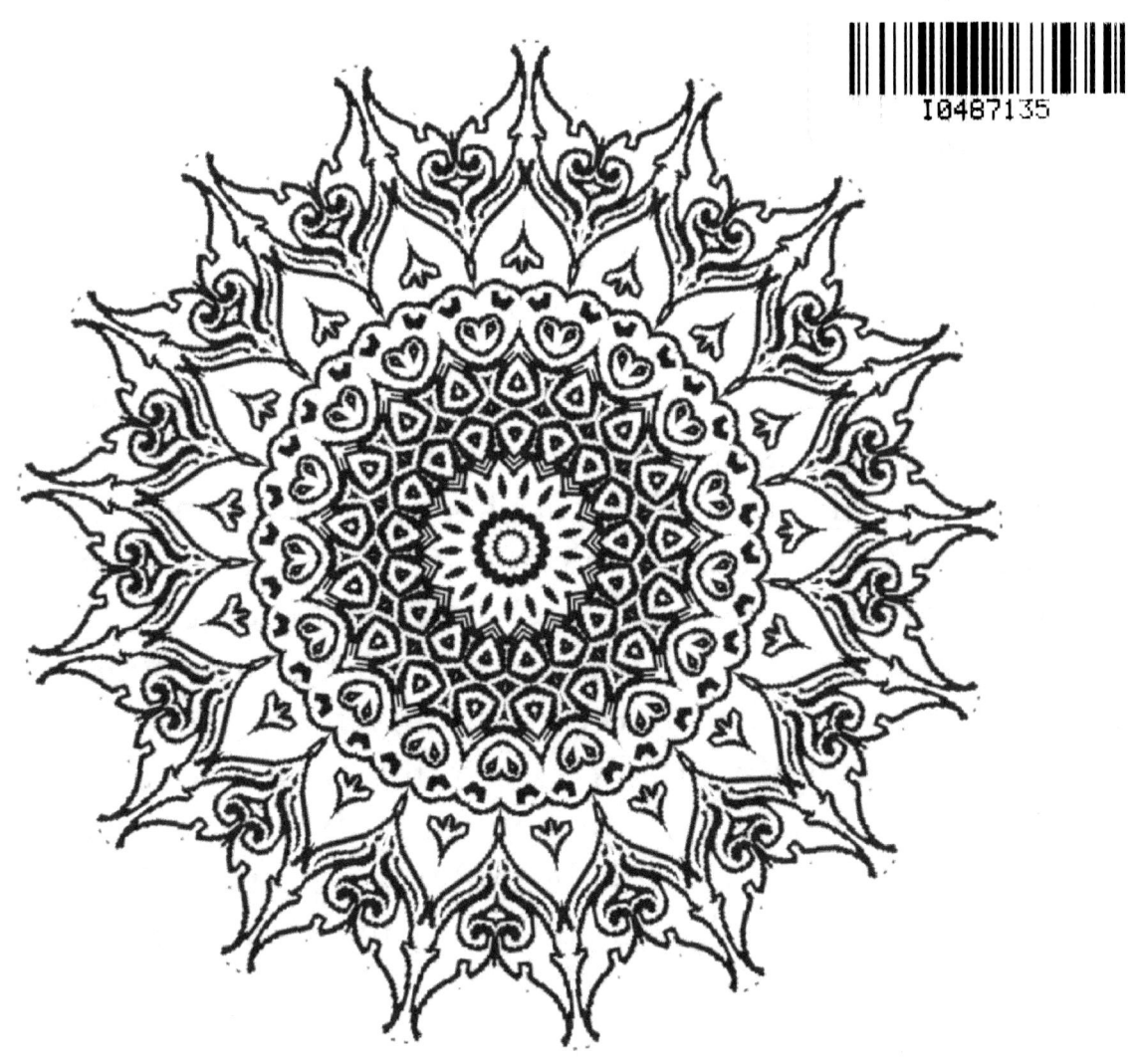

Miracle Coloring Arts

About the Author

Miracle Coloring Arts He liked to draw and paint by his imagination.
Every time he has done it. It made him feel like being in another world.
Feel relaxed, energetic, and wisdom of thinking.
Because of his beliefs about the law of attraction.
If you want to attract all the good things that you want in a good side.
You should maintain the sense to stay on the positive side.
Then focus on what you want.
If you maintain a positive feeling long enough. You will find amazing
things that happen to you.
The art of coloring is one thing that will relax you and pull you into the
idea that as a positive.
Hope you enjoyed with it.

Disclaimer

All the material contained in this book is provided for educational and informational purposes only. No responsibility can be taken for any results or outcomes resulting from the use of this material.

While every attempt has been made to provide information that is both accurate and effective, the author does not assume any responsibility for the accuracy or use/misuse of this information.

How to use this book
Let's Color

1. Prepare the equipment you will use, such as paint, crayons or other as you like.

2. Find the peace place without interference from other things.

3. Leave the thinking to independence. Disregard the Past and a future that is yet to come. Focus the current only.

4. Tinged with relax

The Meaning of Colors

Red = the color of energy, passion, action, ambition and determination.

Orange = the color of social communication and optimism.

Yellow = the color of sunshine. It's associated with joy, happiness, intellect, and energy.

Green = the color of balance and growth.

Blue = the color of trust and peace.

Indigo = the color of intuition.

Purple = the color of the imagination.

Turquoise = the color of communication and clarity of mind.

Pink = the color of unconditional love and nurturing.

Magenta = the color of universal harmony and emotional balance.

Brown = the color of friendly.

Gray = the color of compromise.

Silver = the color of feminine energy. It is related to the moon and the ebb and flow of the tides - it is fluid, emotional, sensitive and mysterious.

Gold = the color of success, achievement and triumph. Associated with abundance and prosperity, luxury and quality, prestige and sophistication, value and elegance.

White = the color of complete and pure, the color of perfection. The color meaning of white is purity, innocence, wholeness and completion.

Black = the color of the hidden, the secretive and the unknown, creating an air of mystery. It keeps things bottled up inside, hidden from the world.

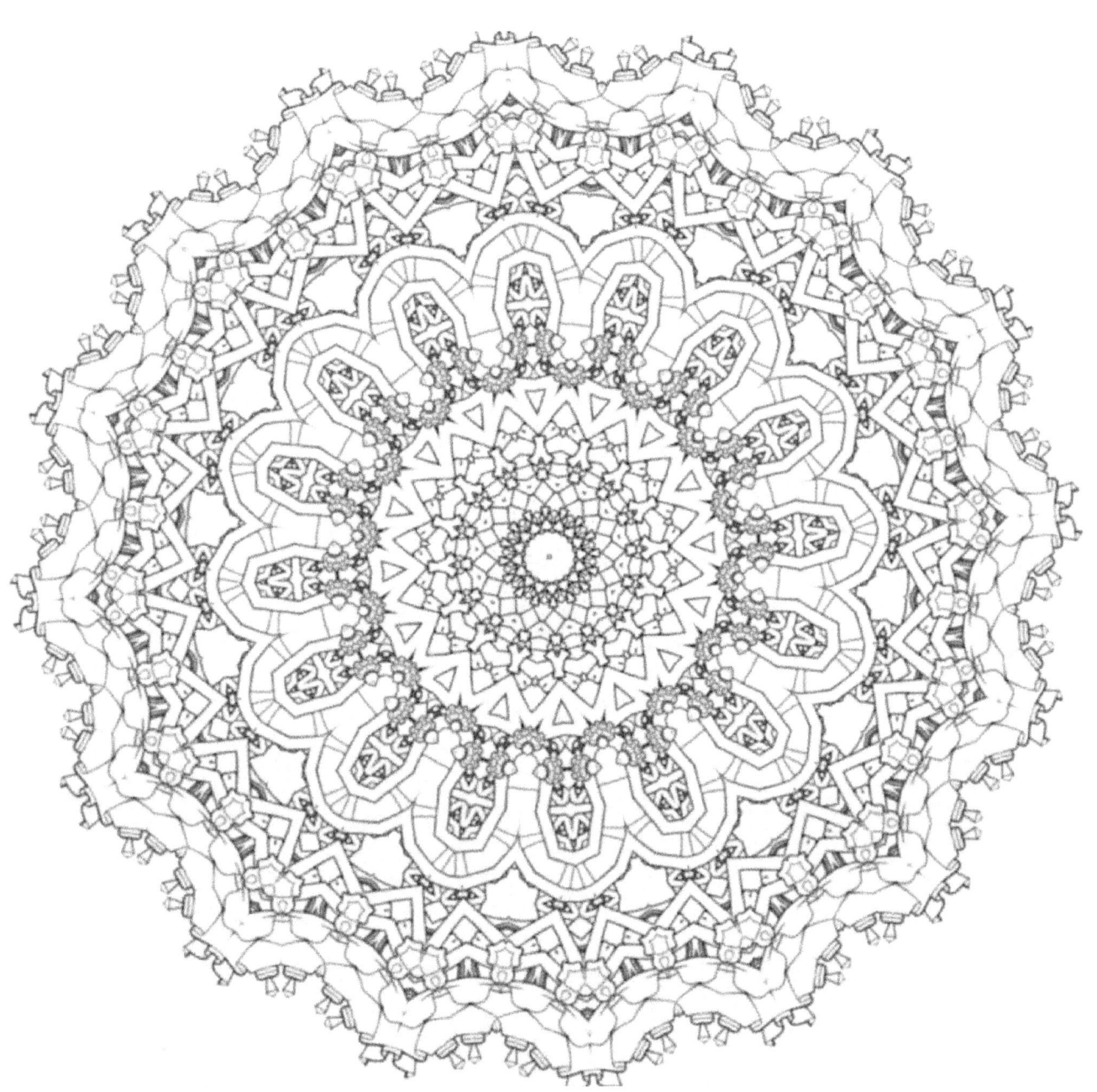

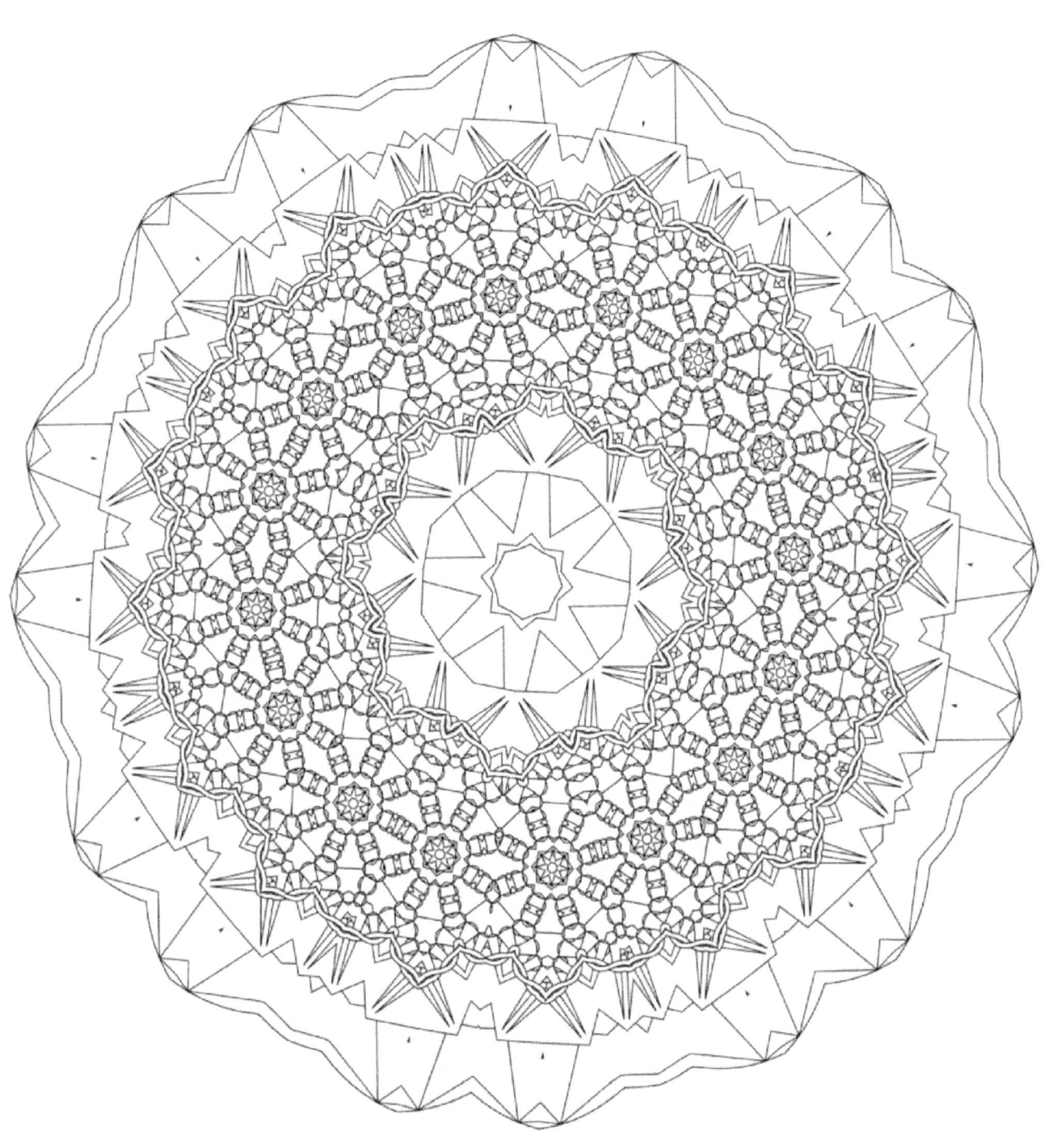

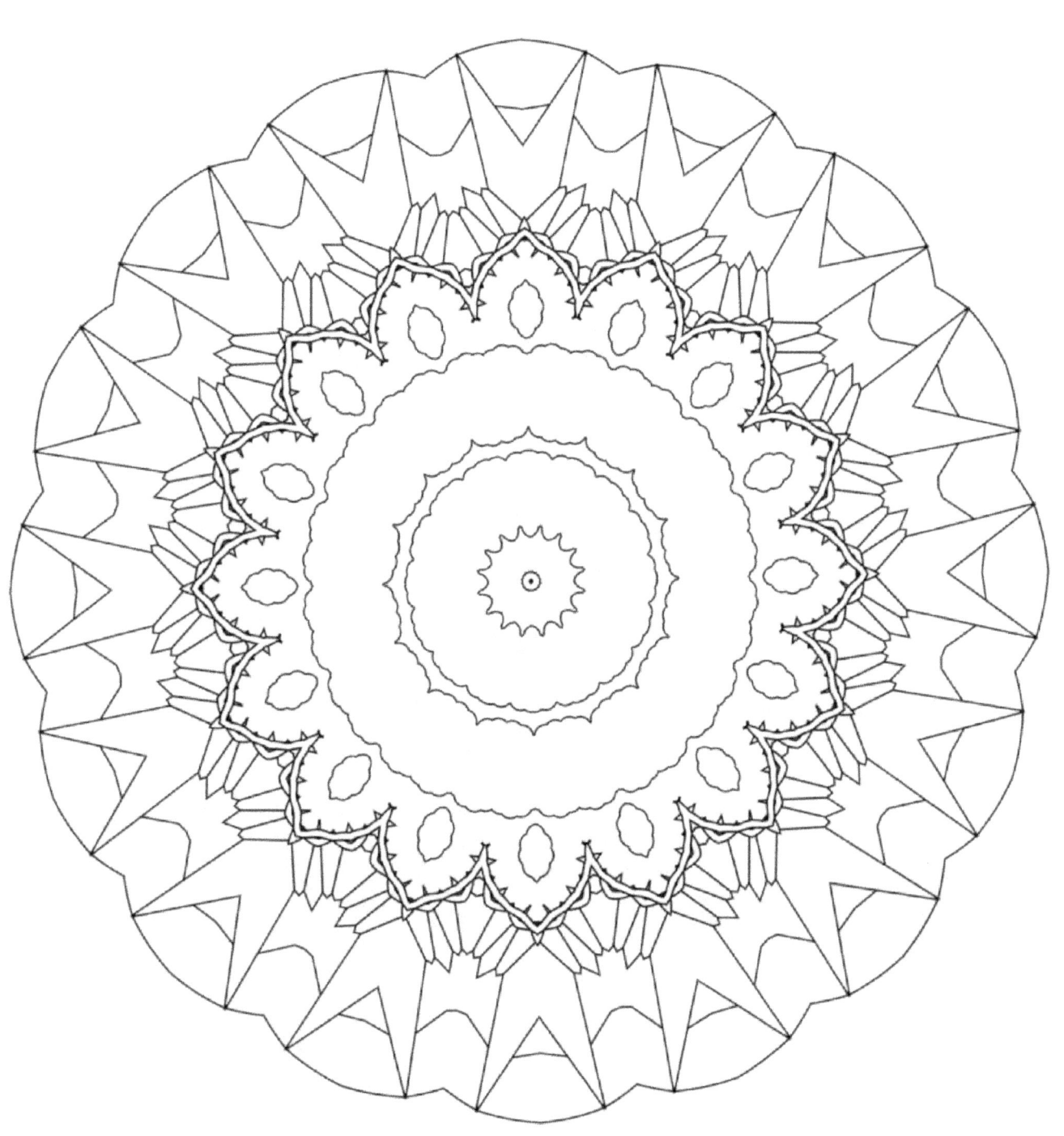

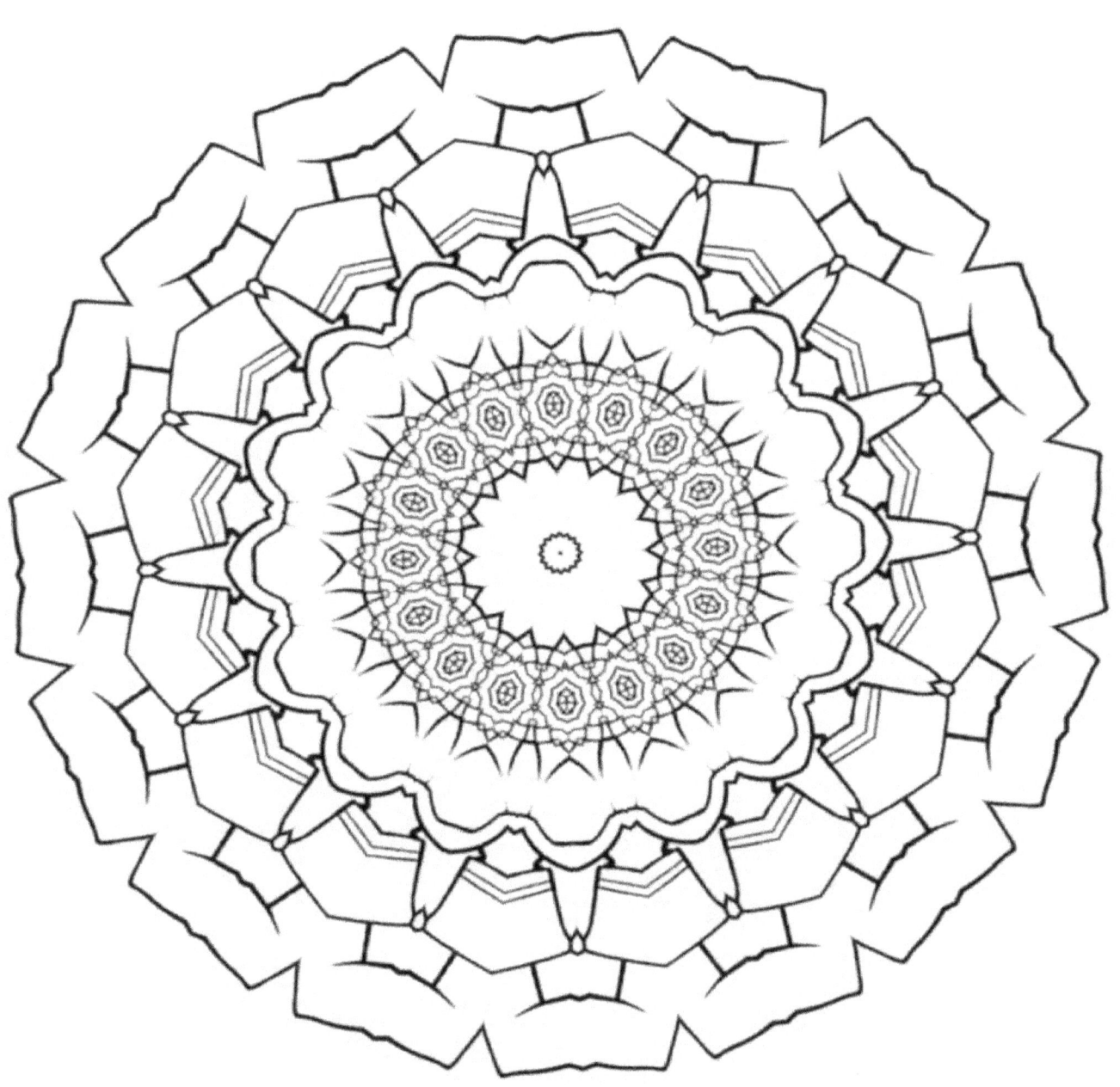

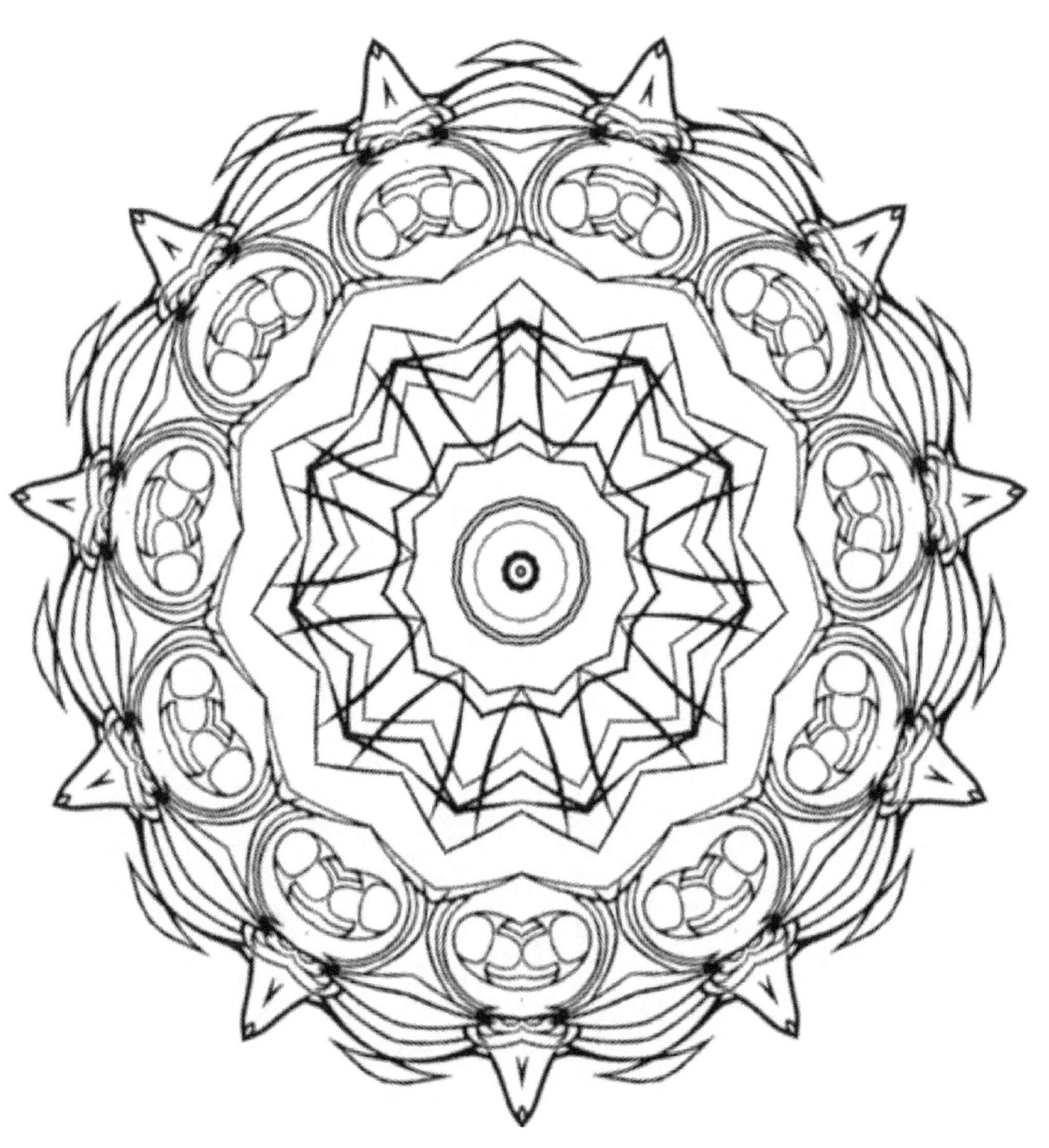

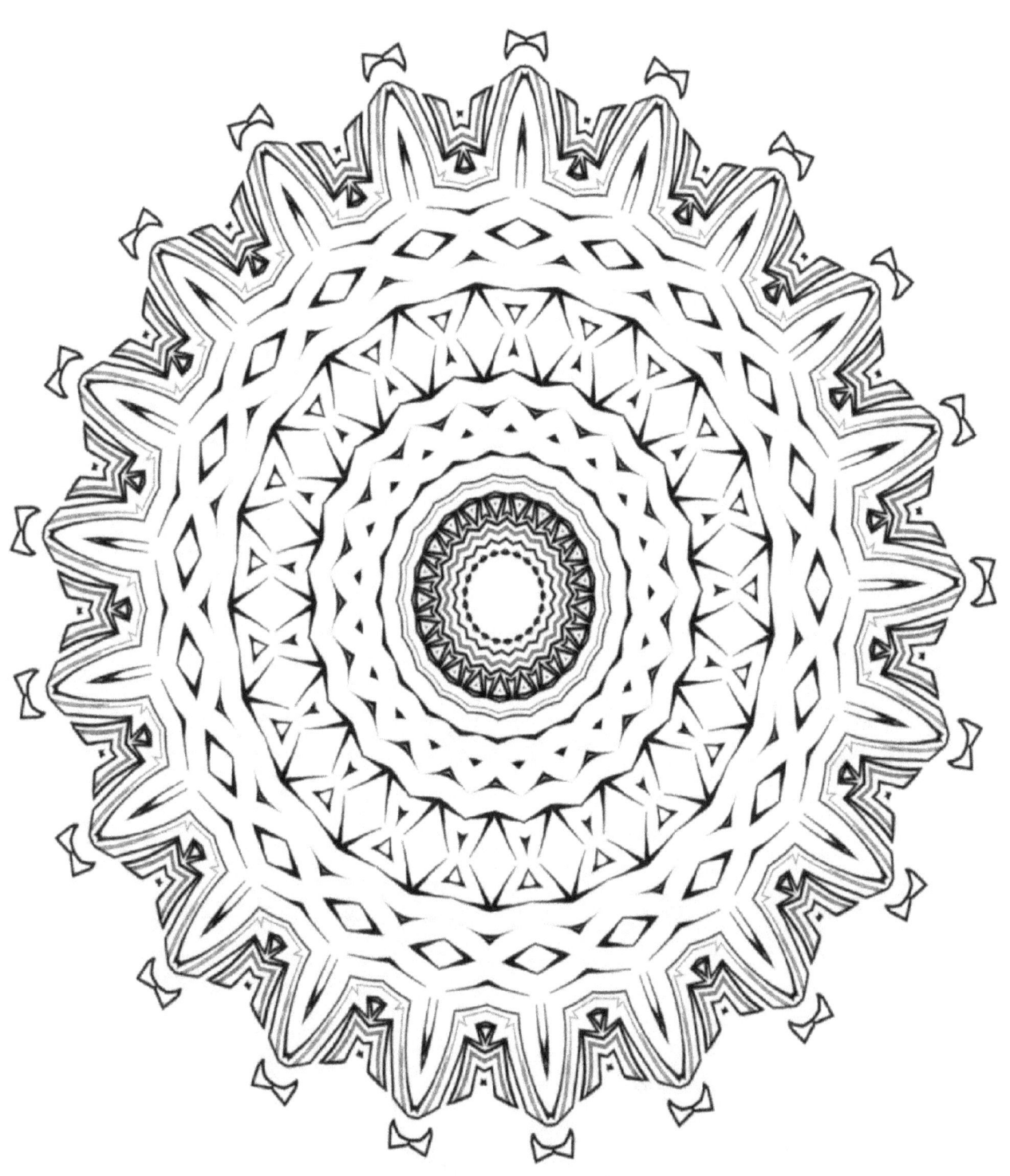

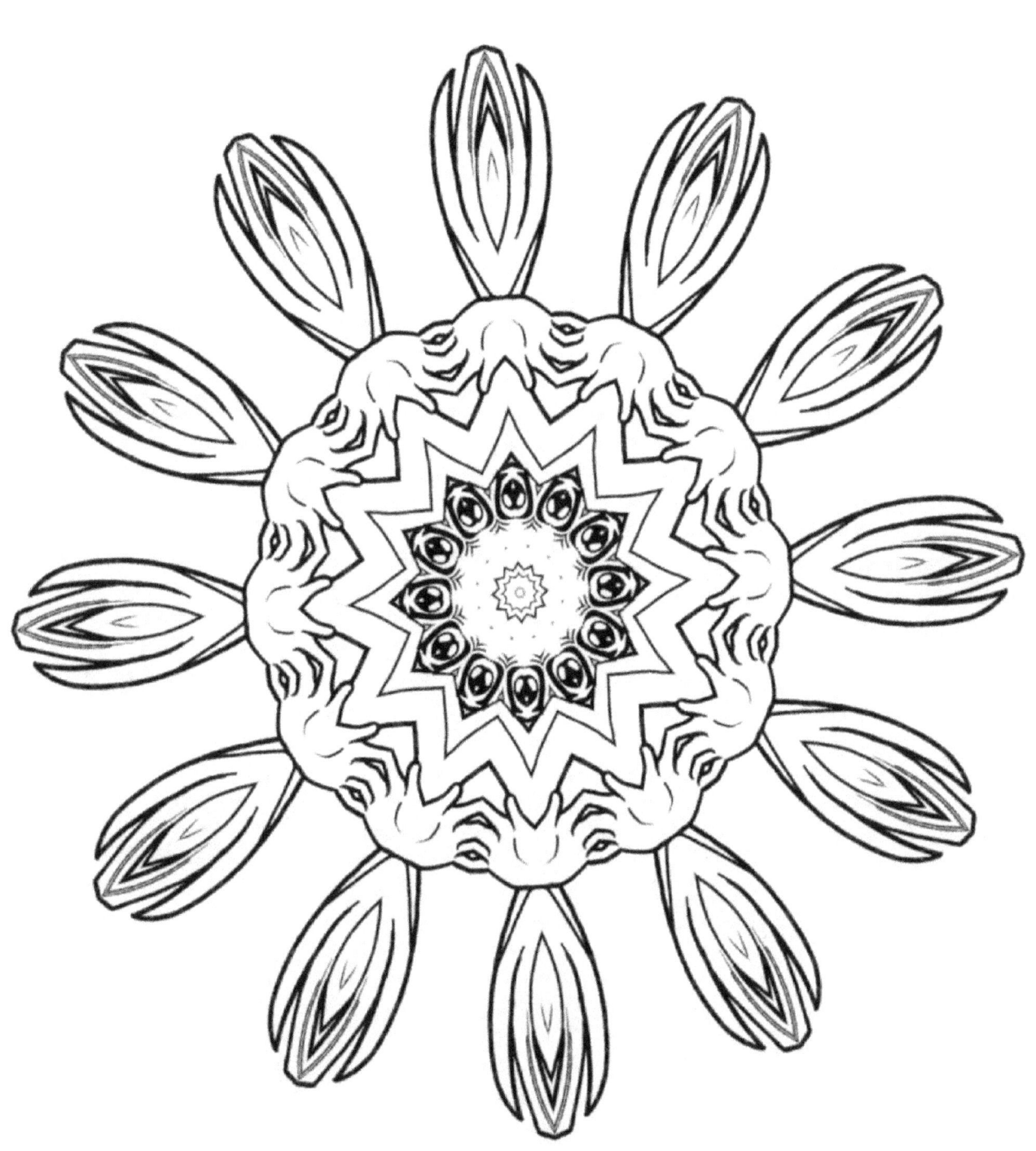

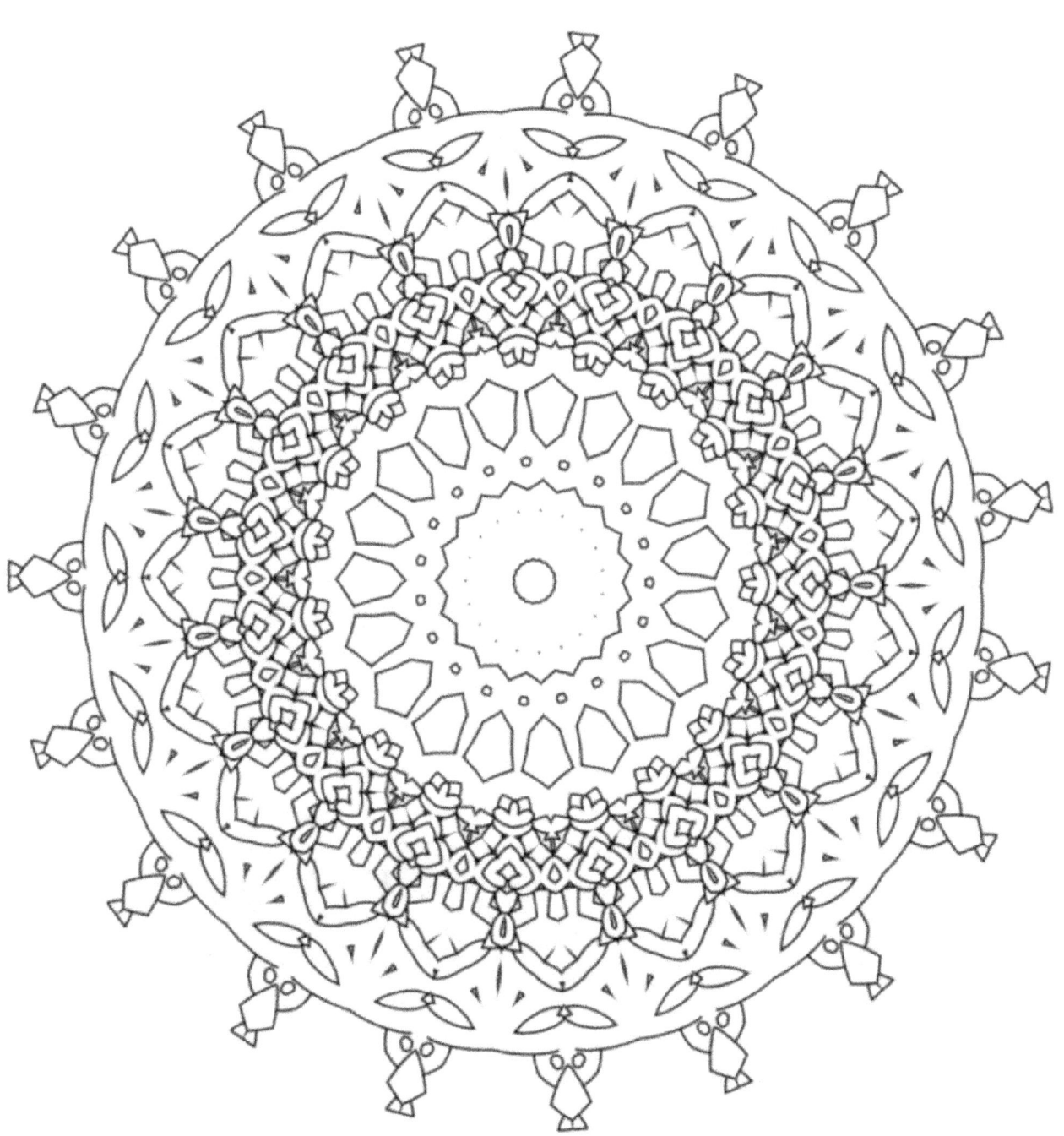

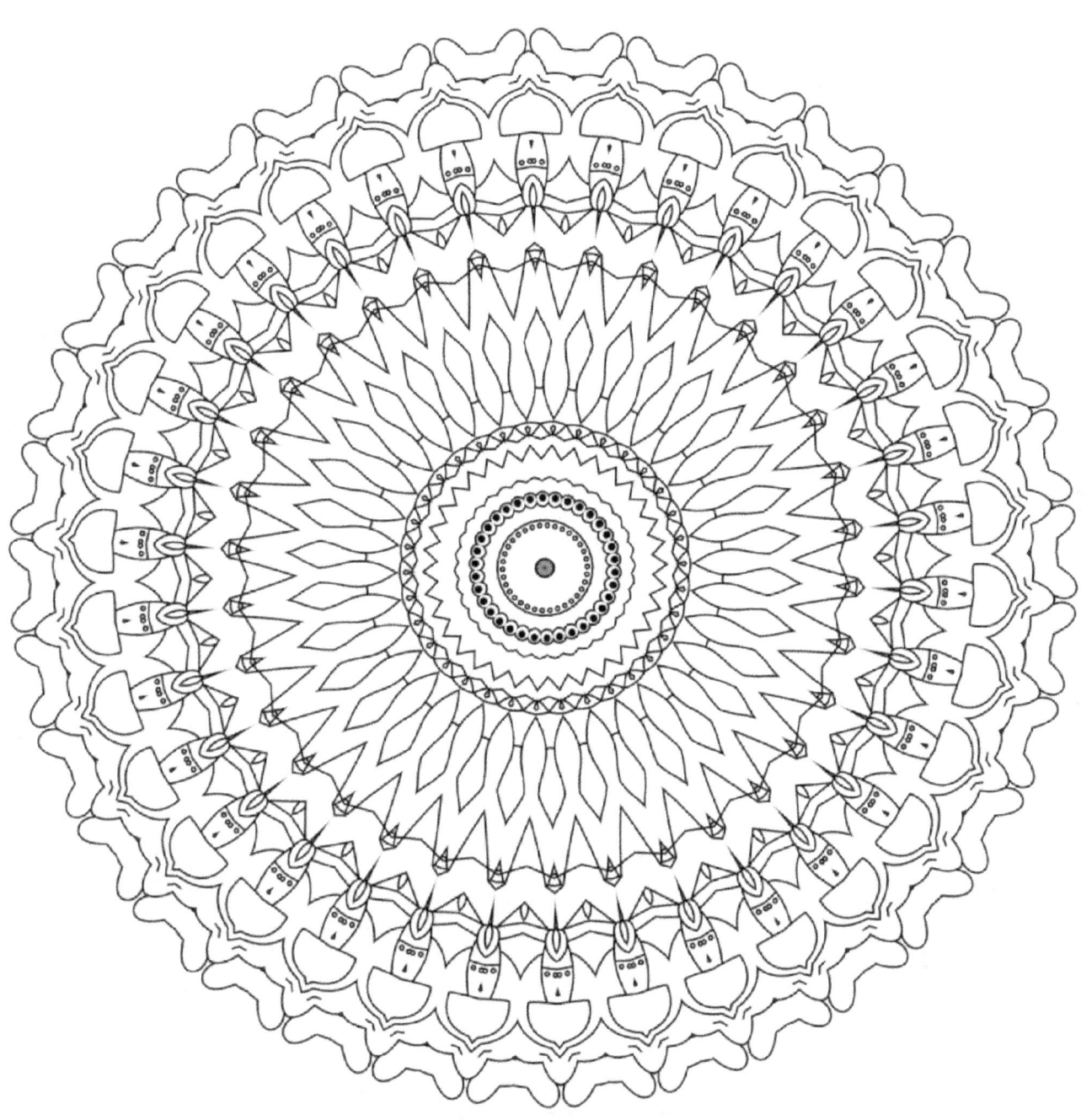

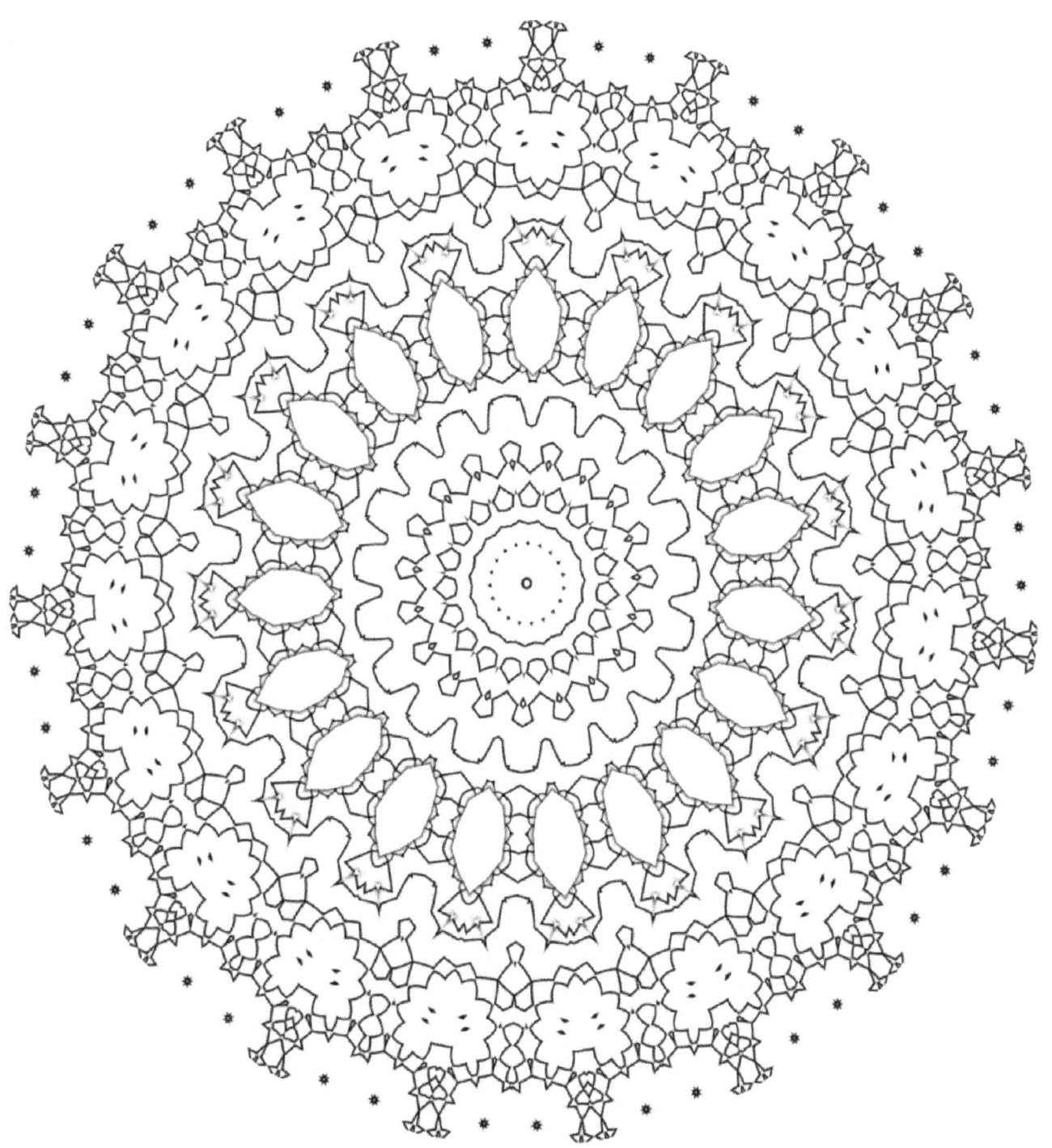

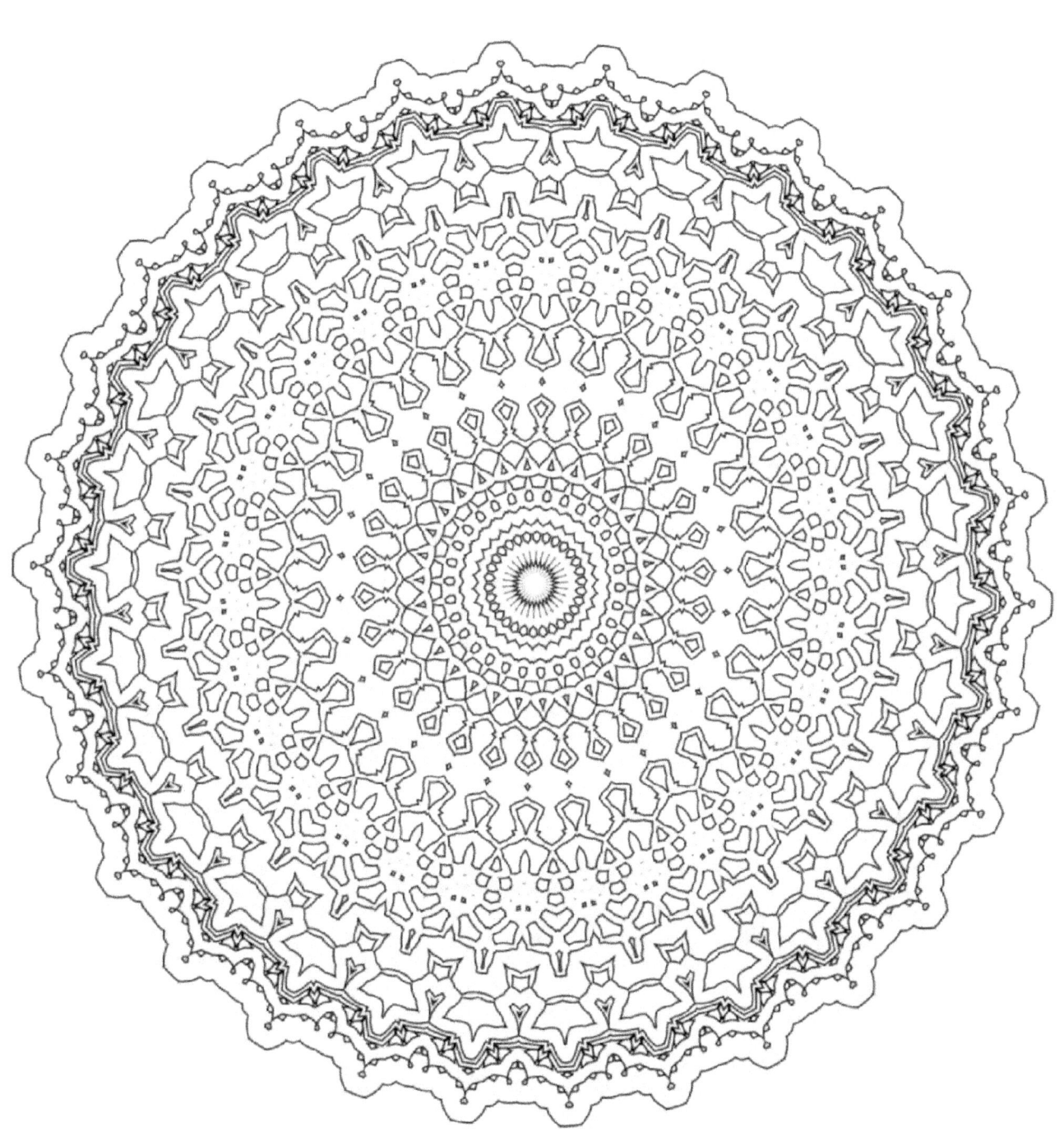

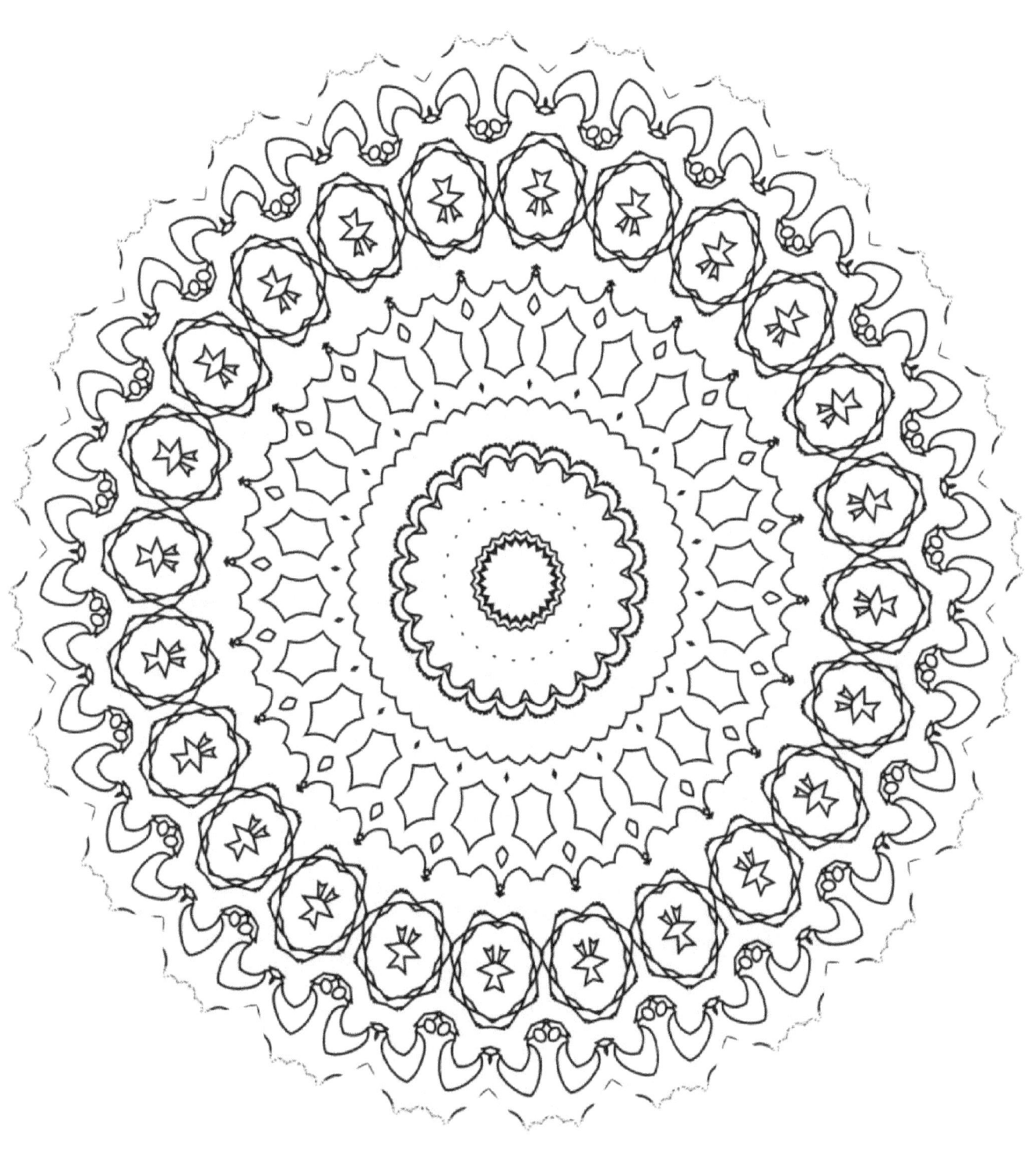

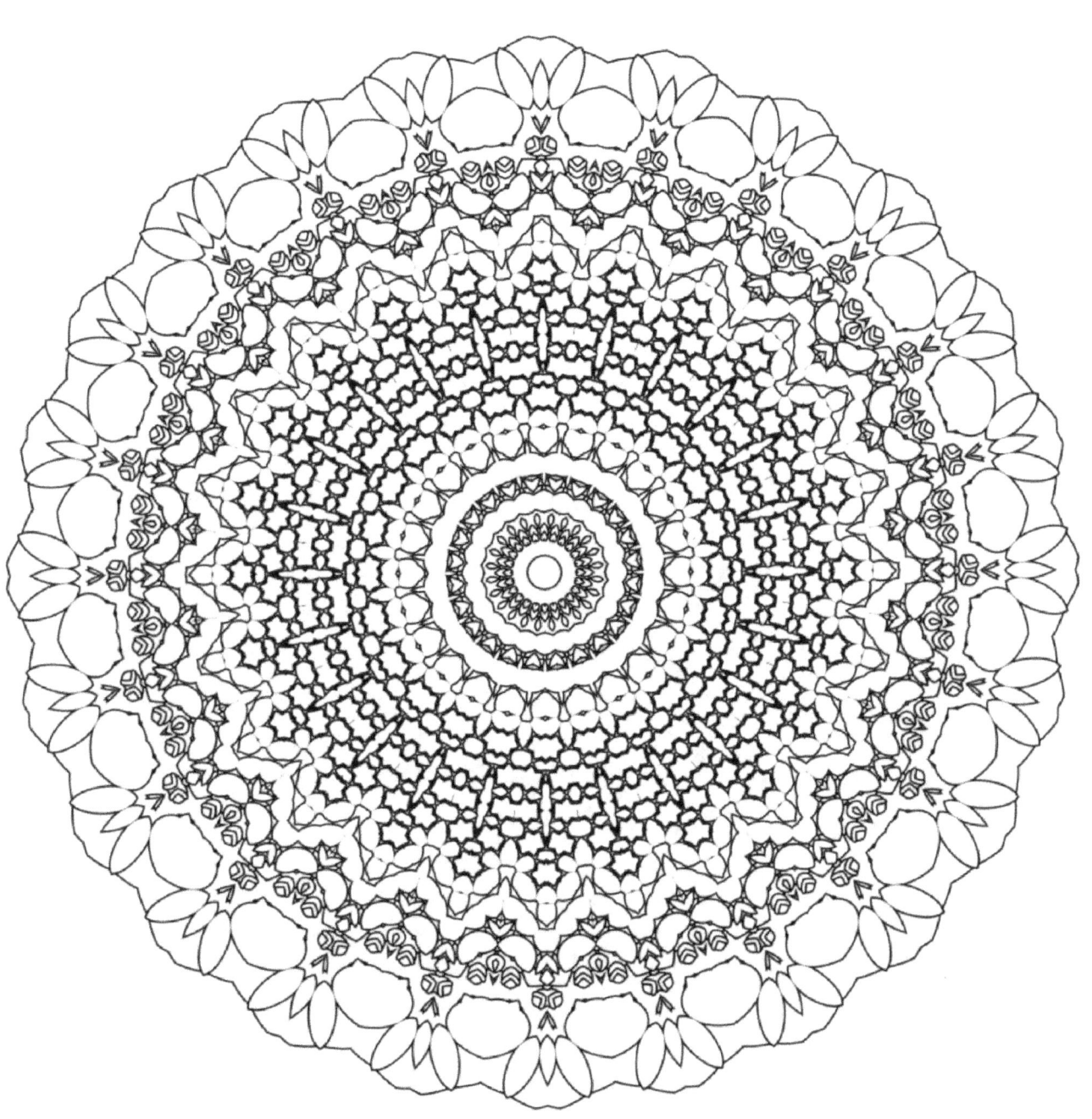

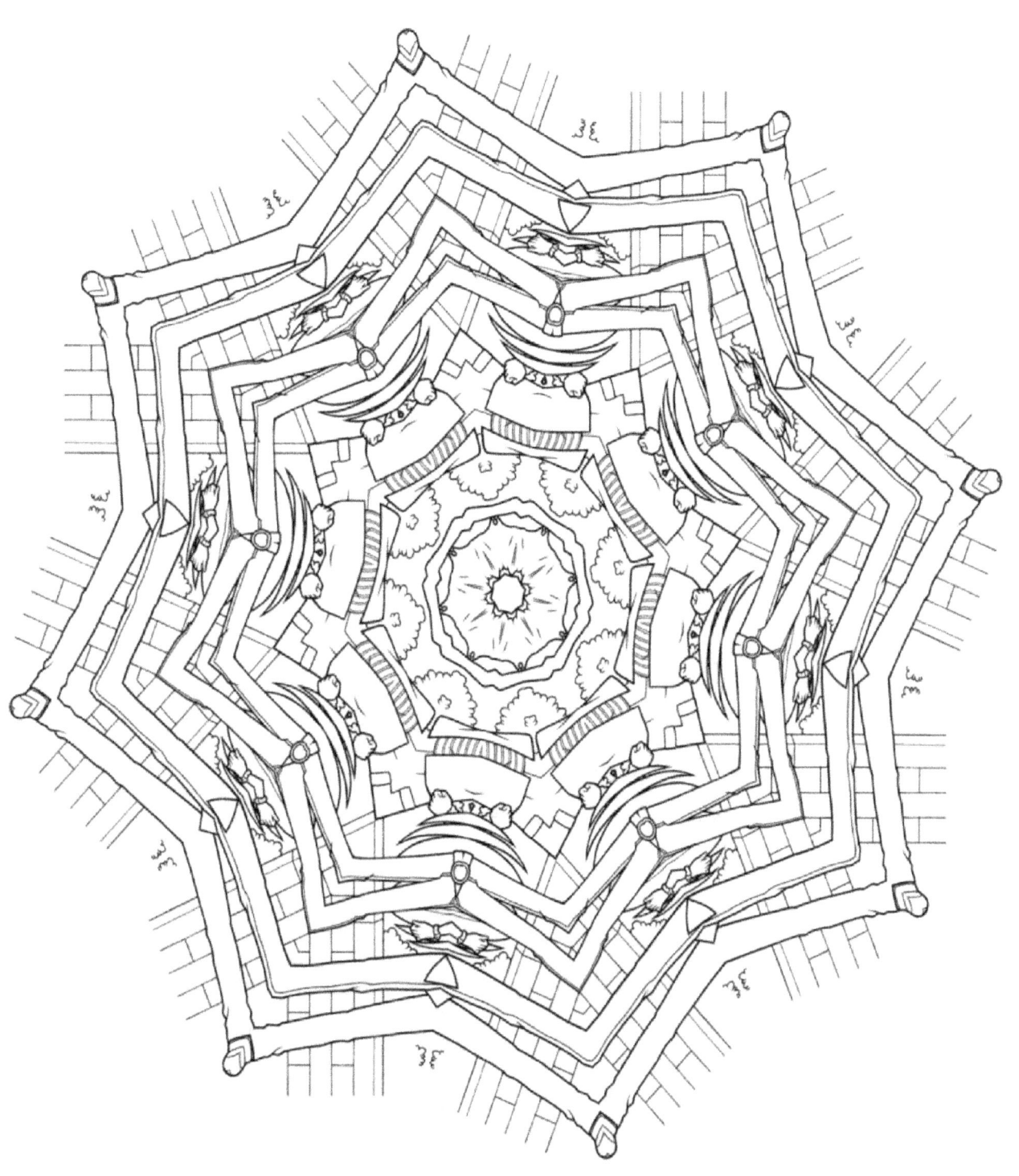

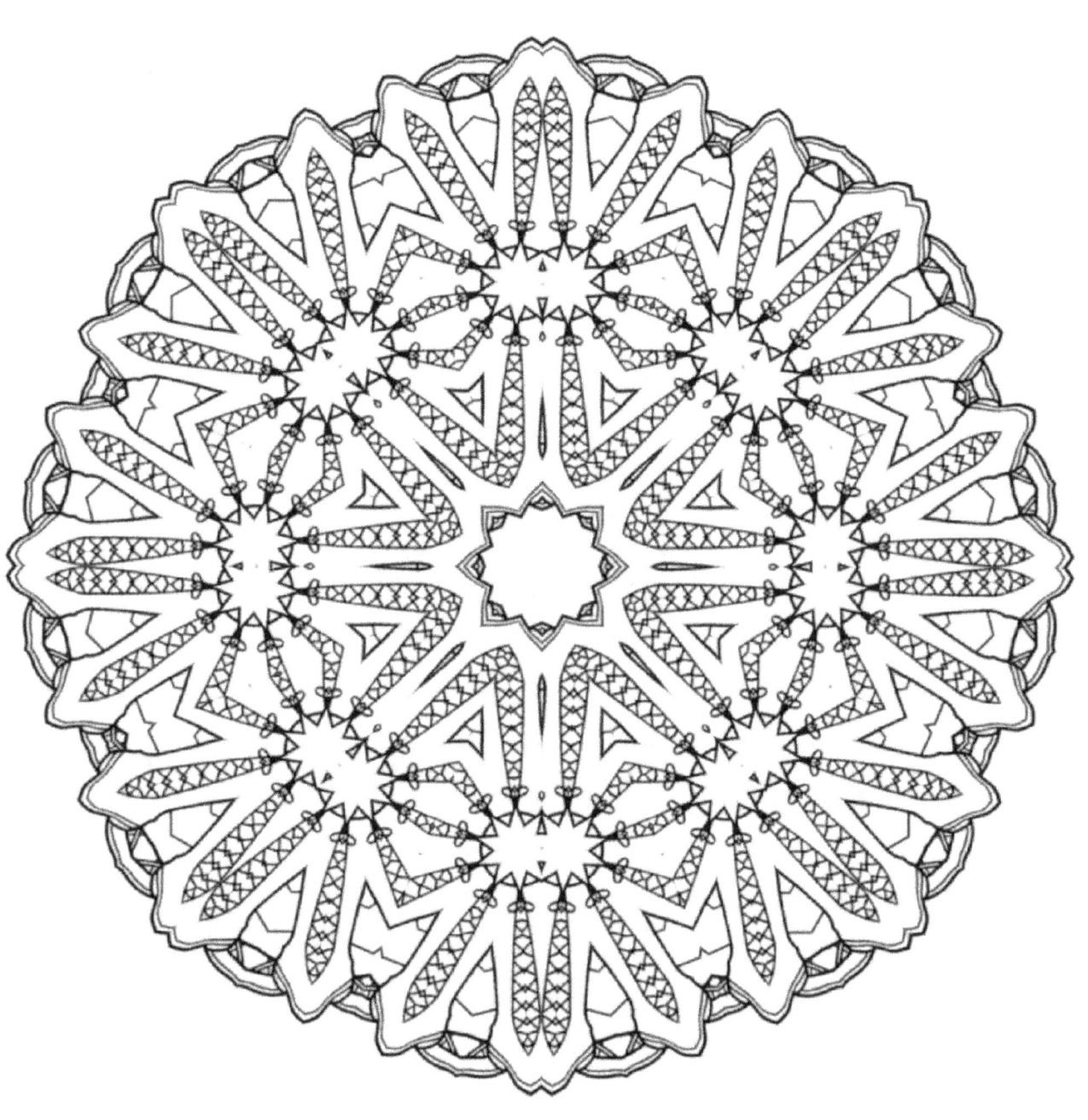

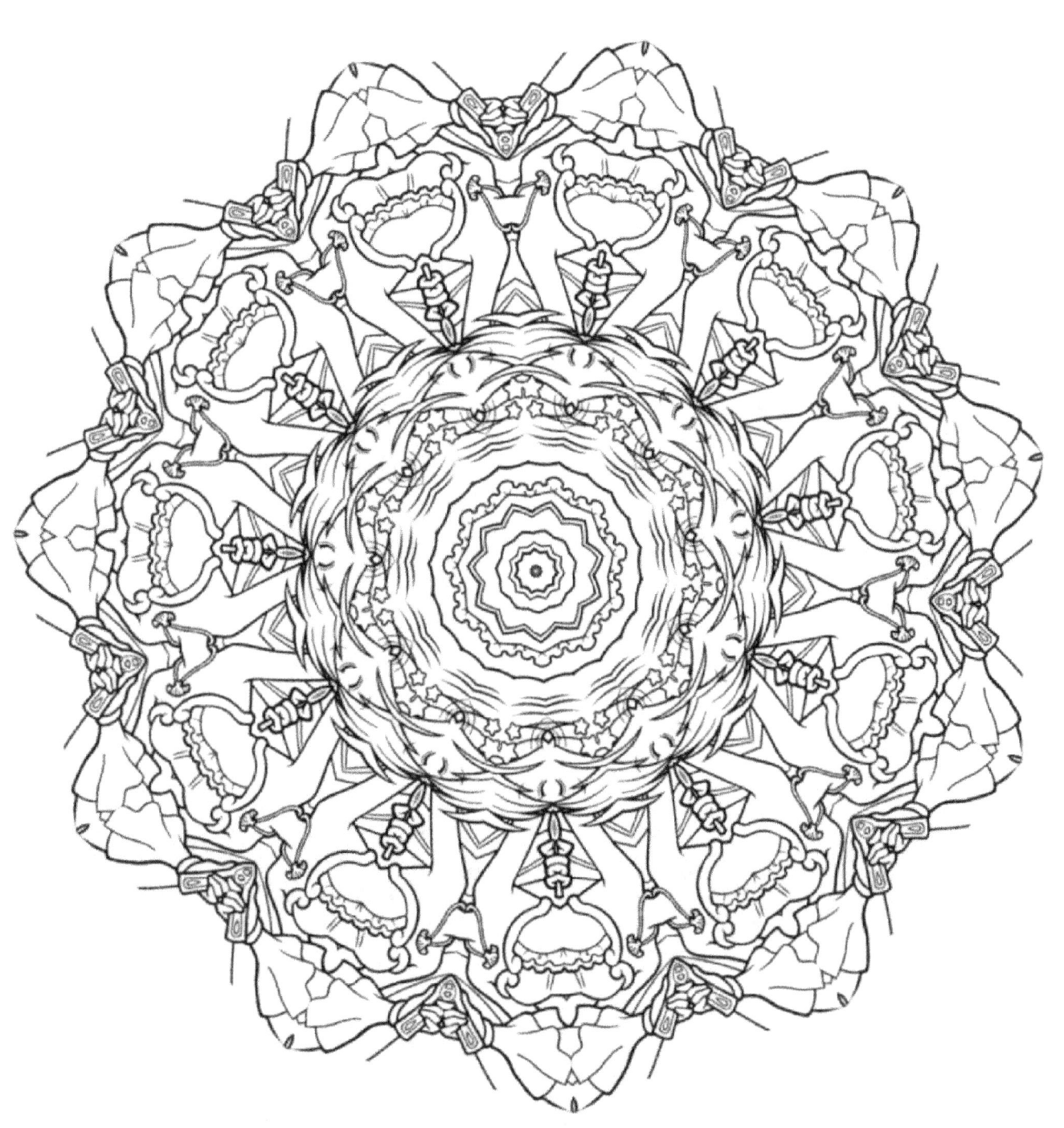

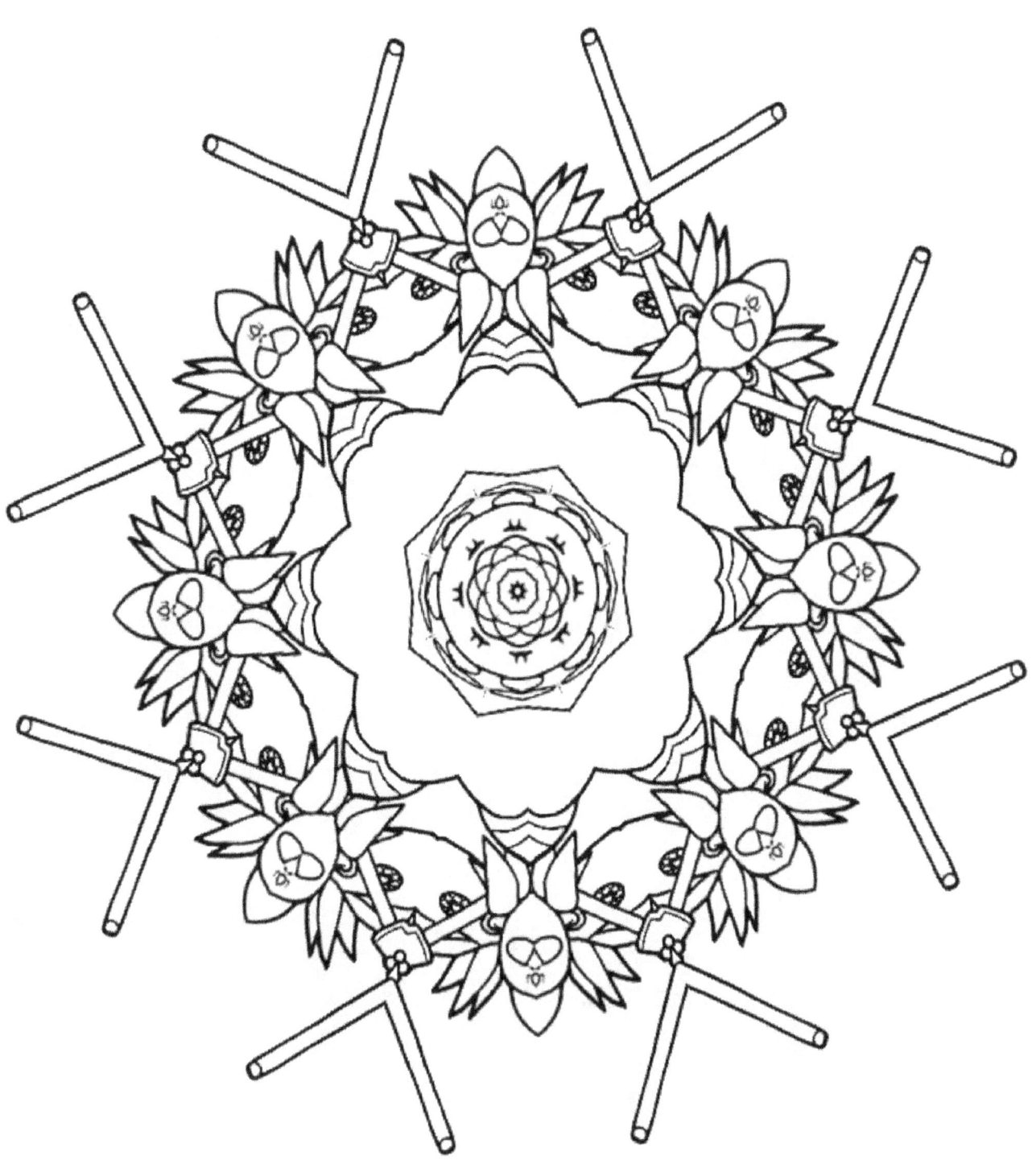

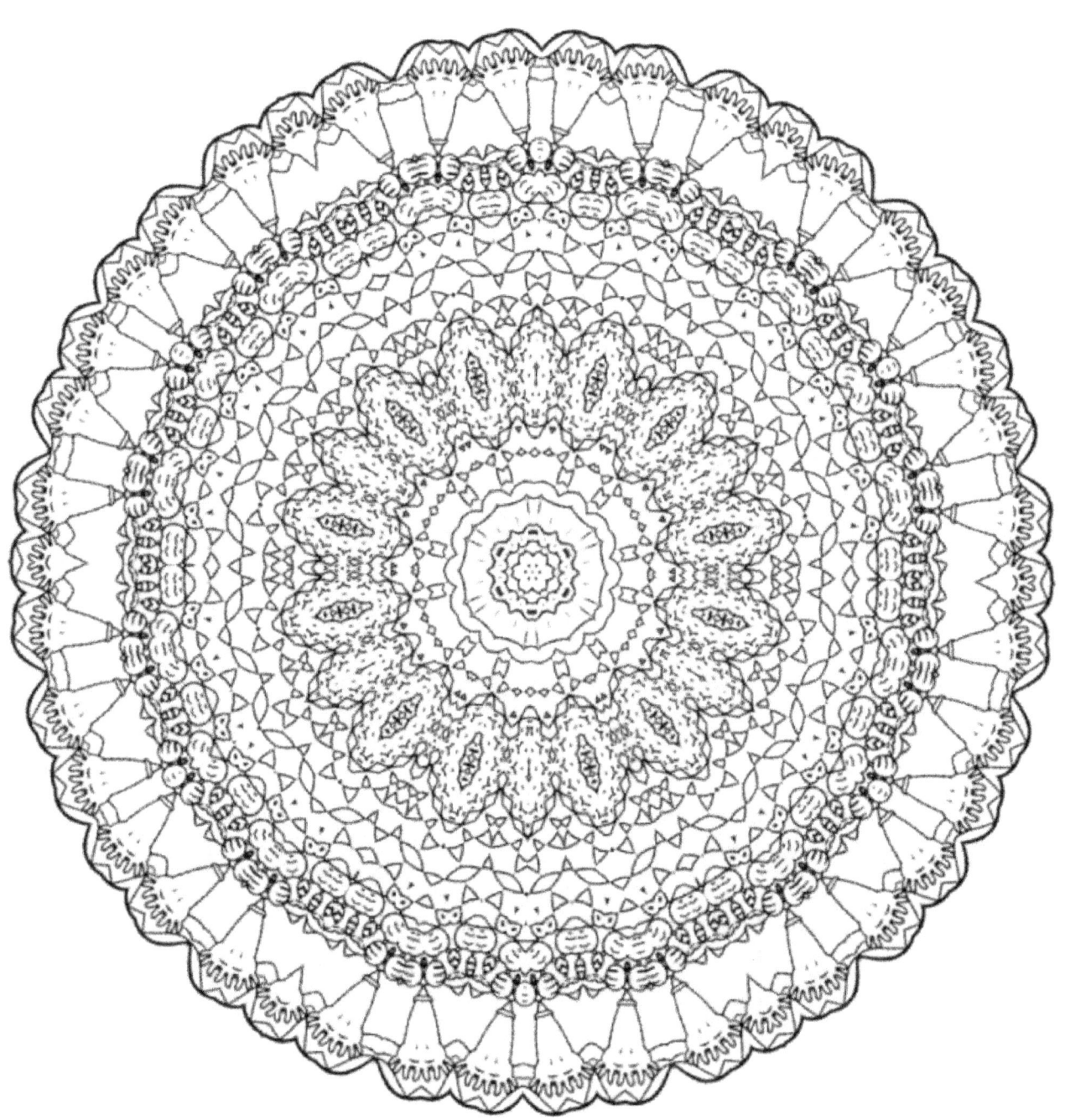

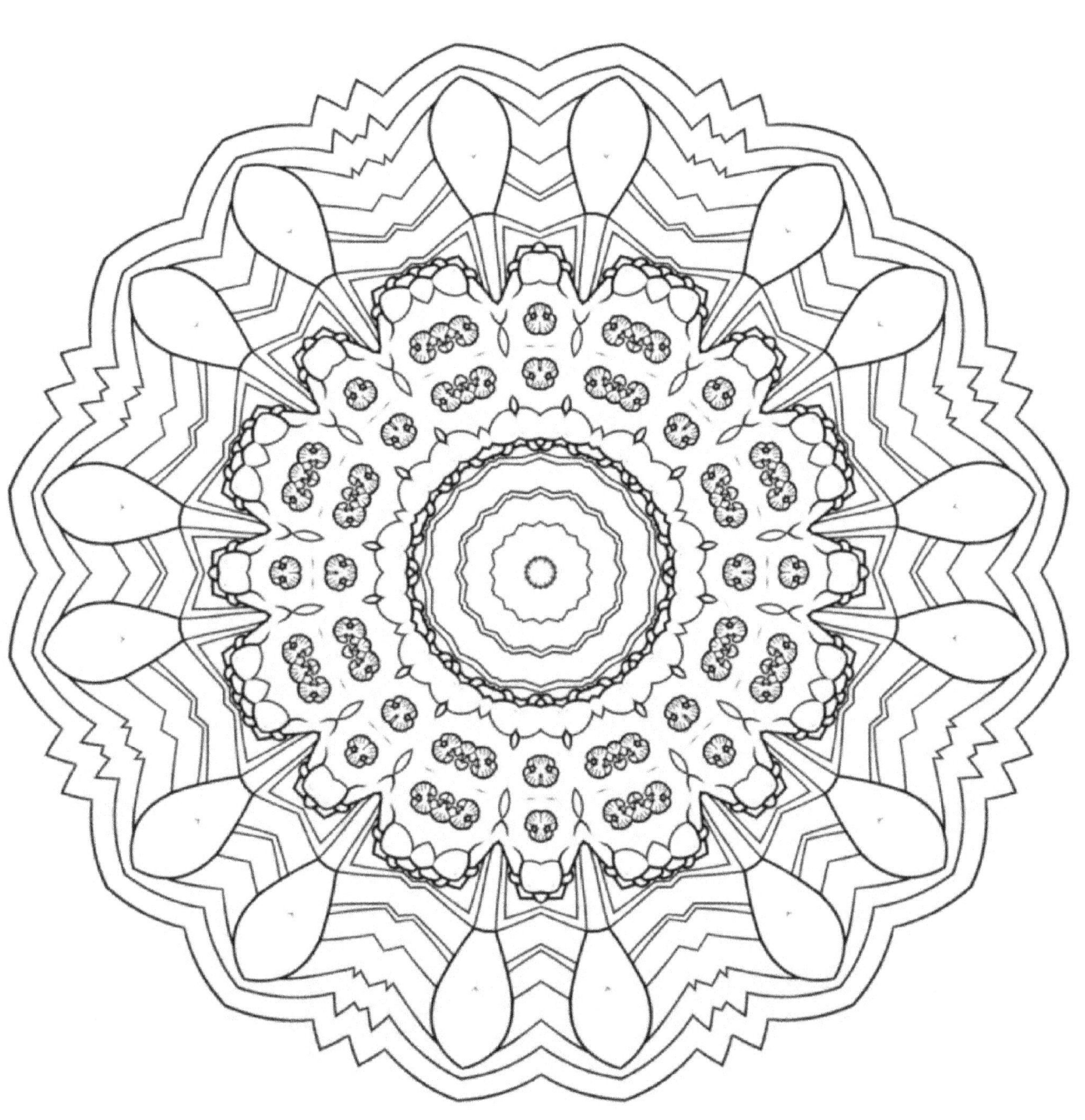

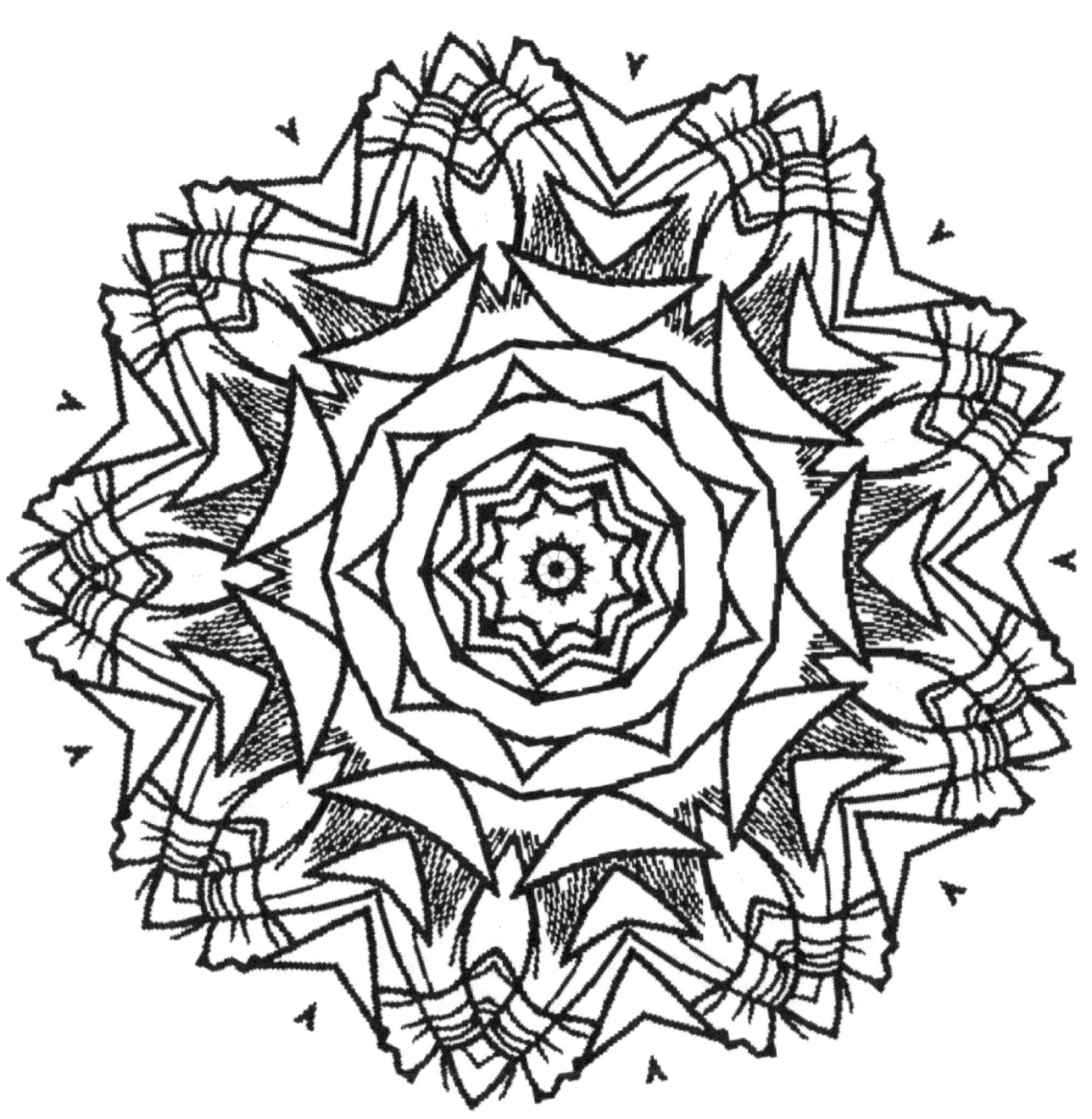

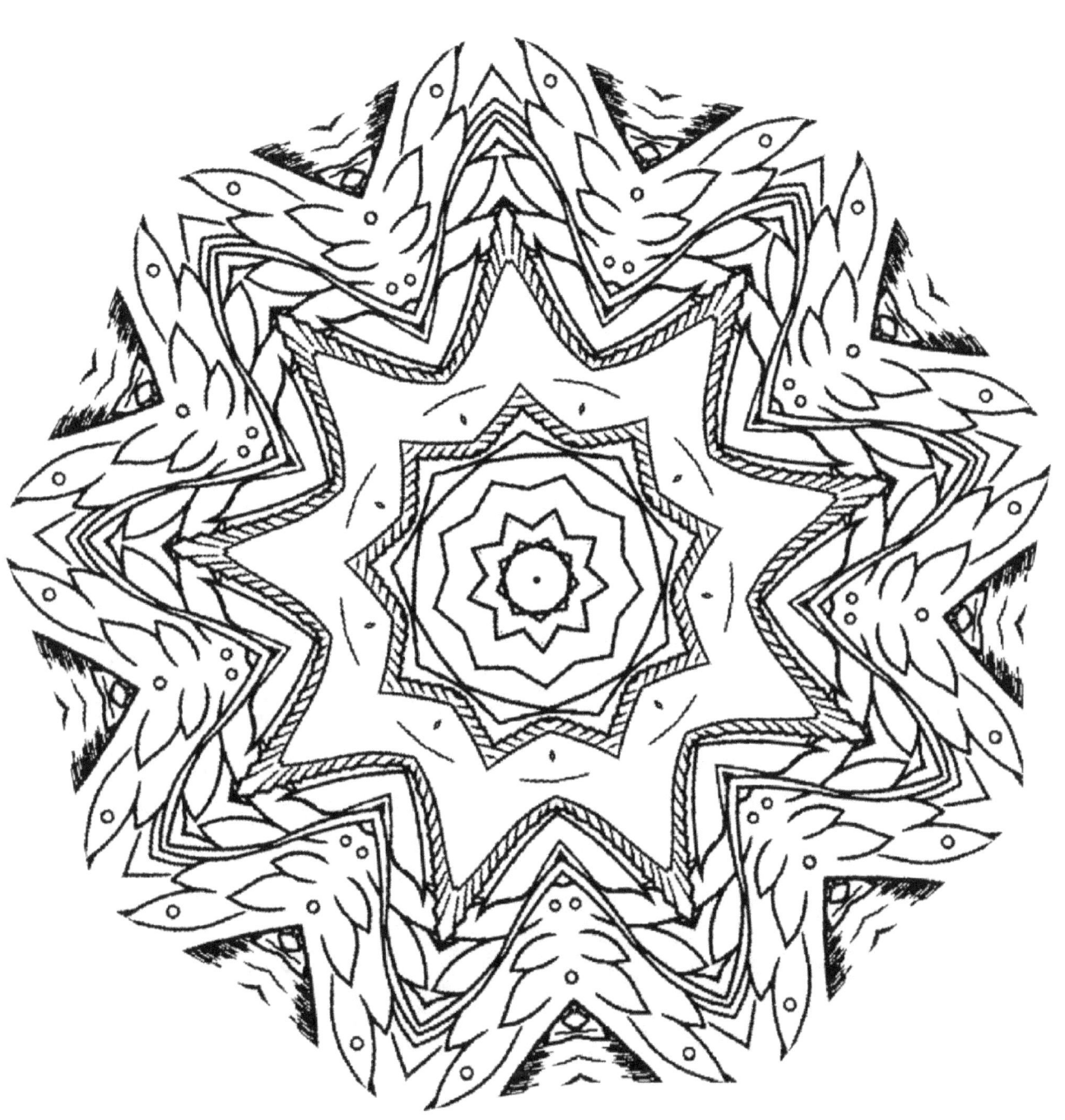

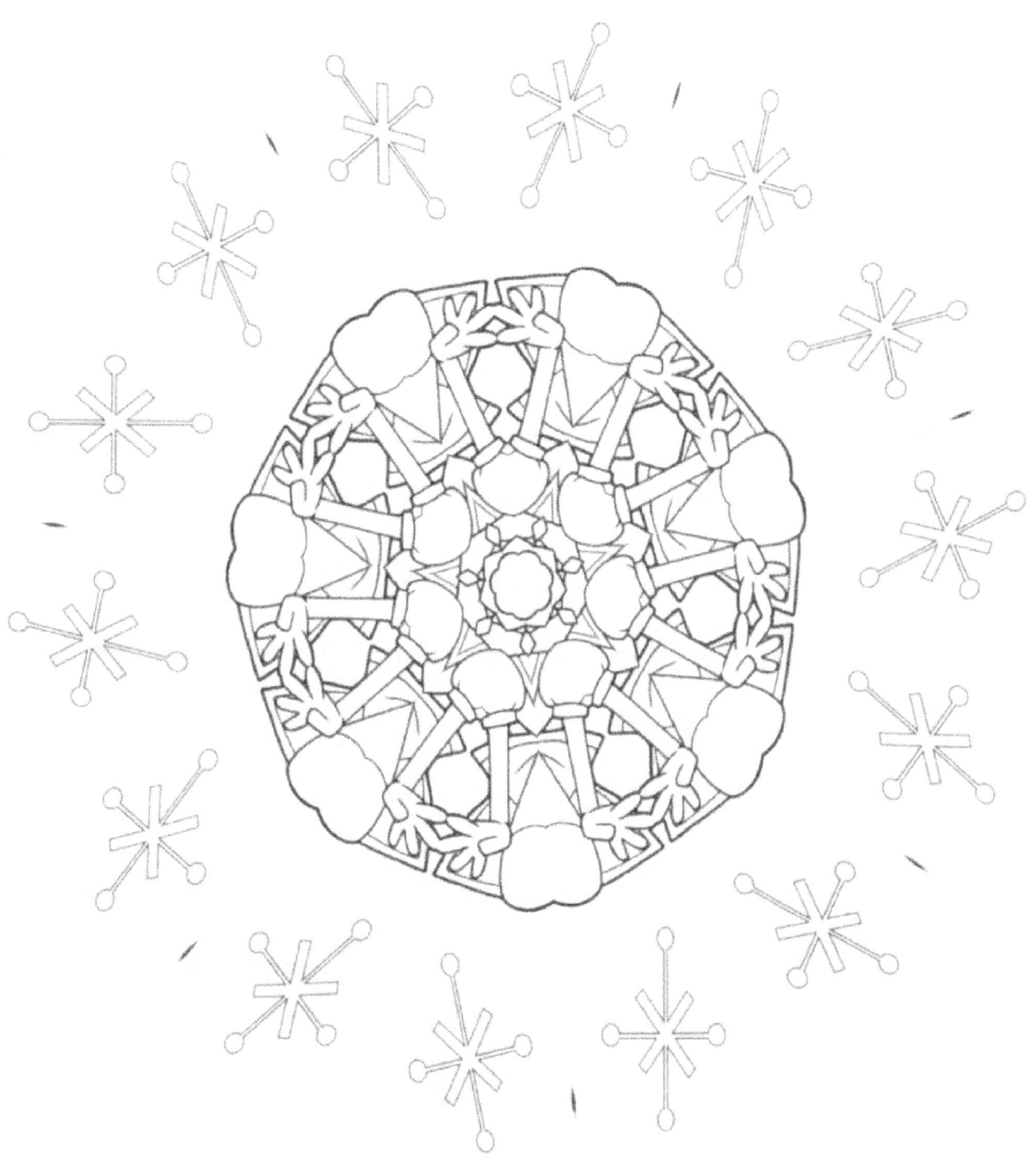

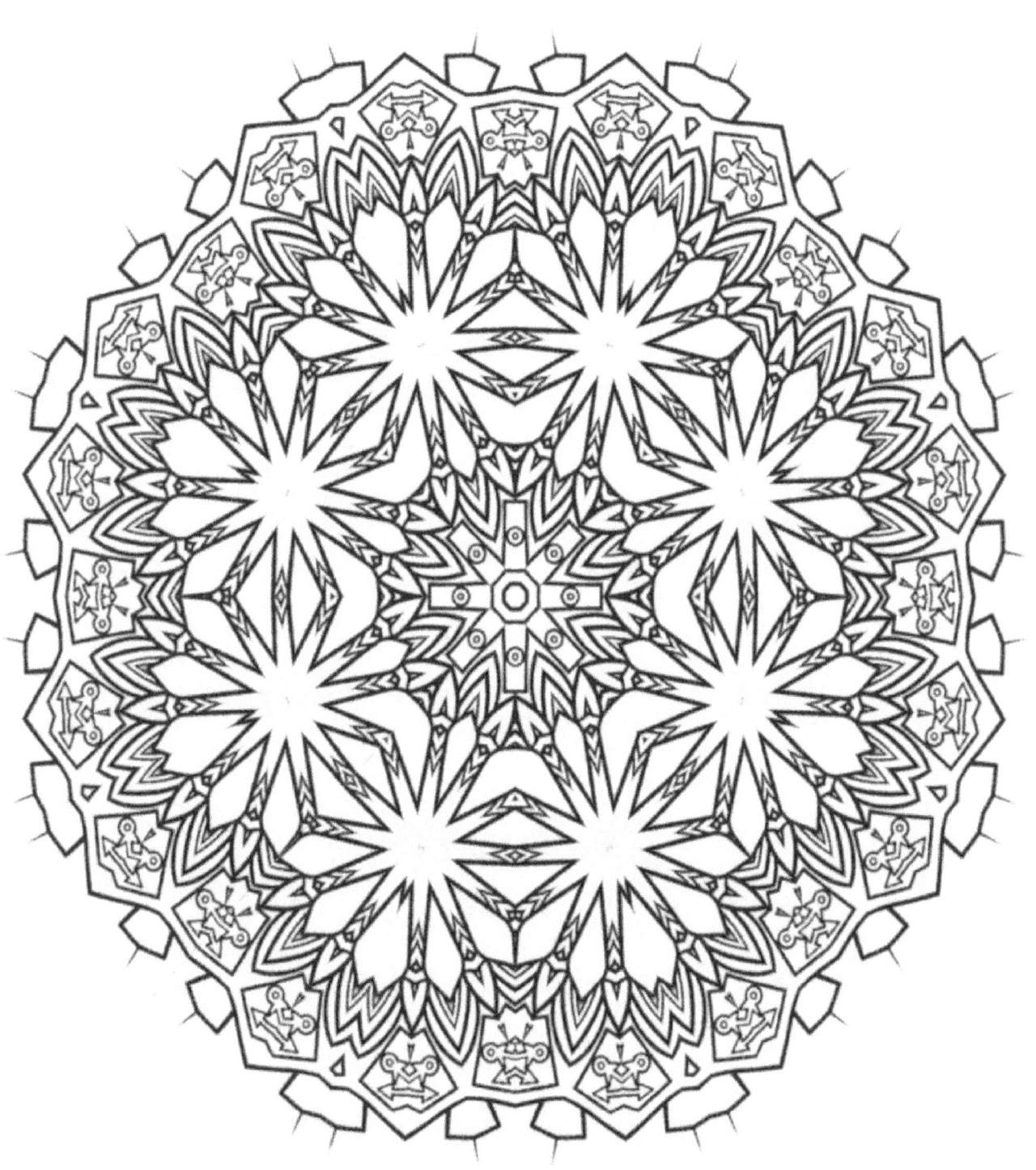

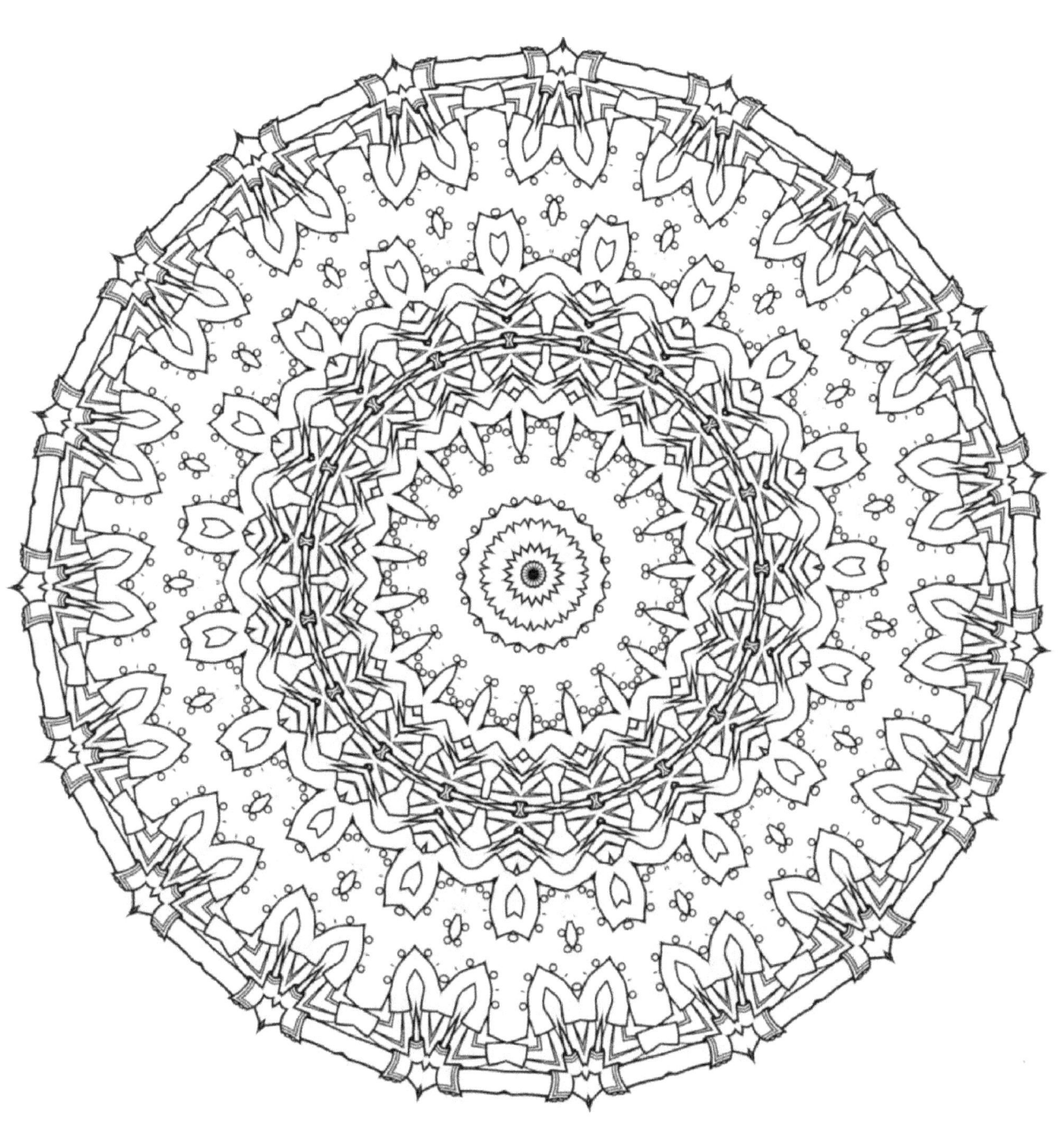

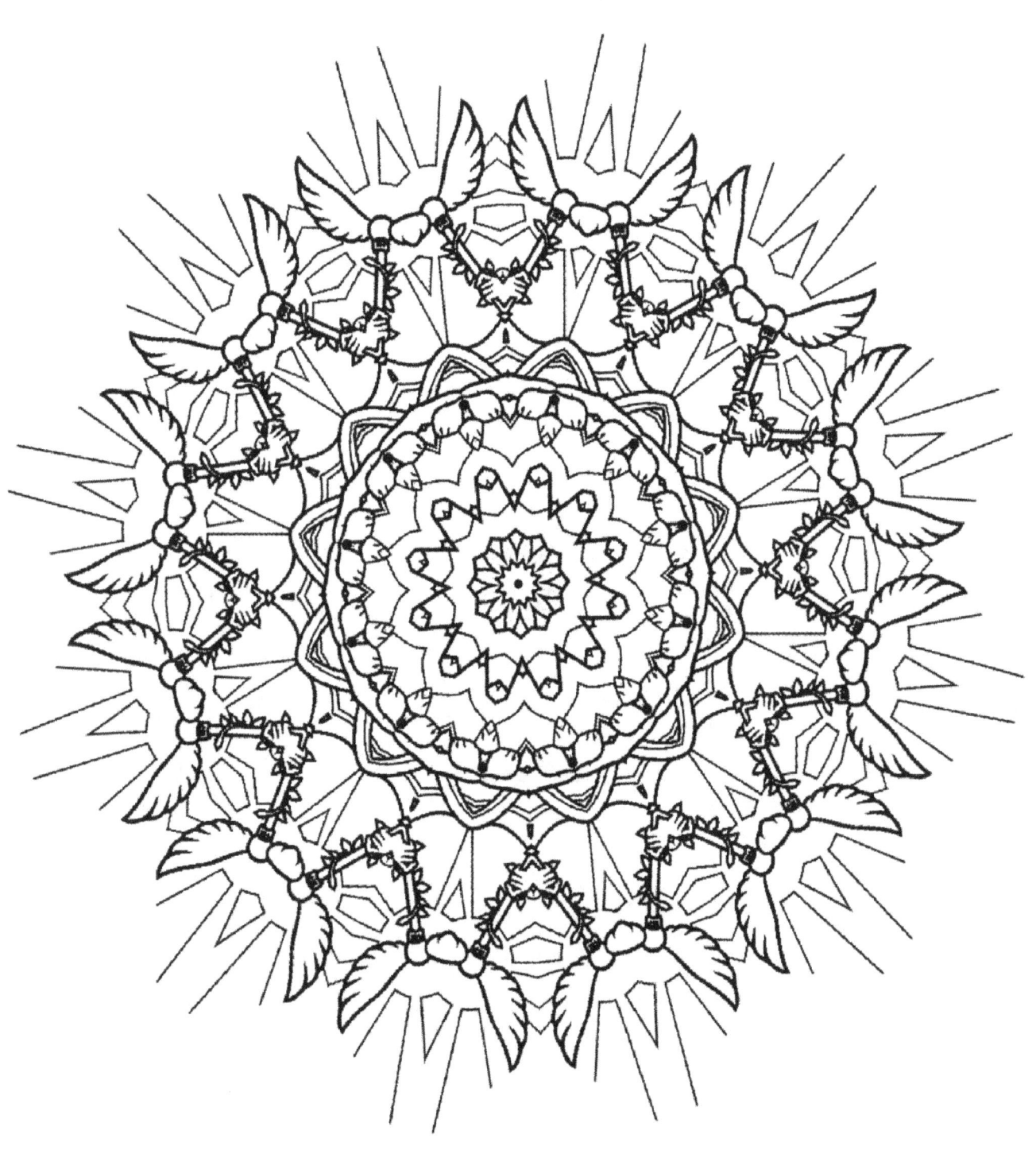

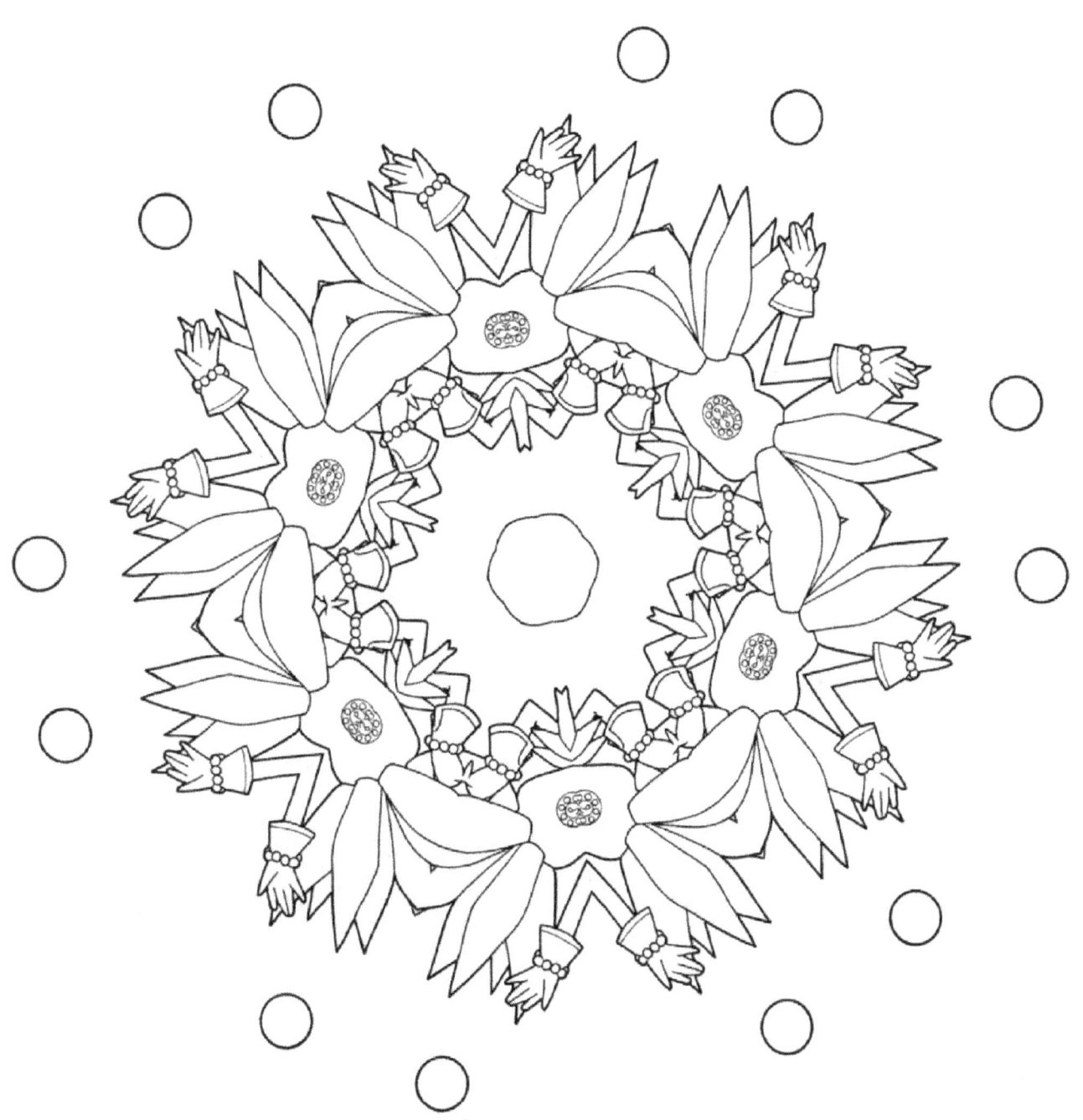

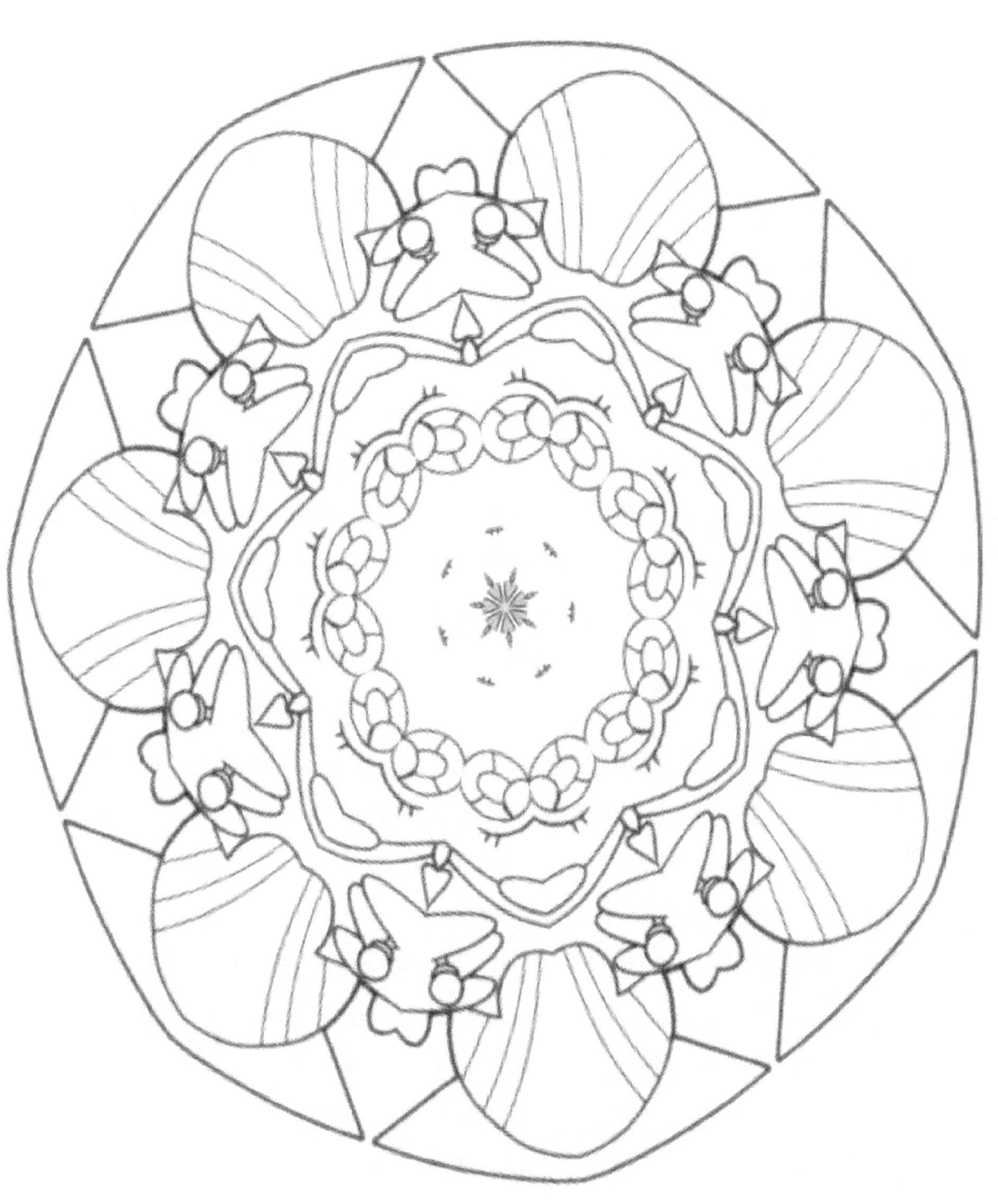

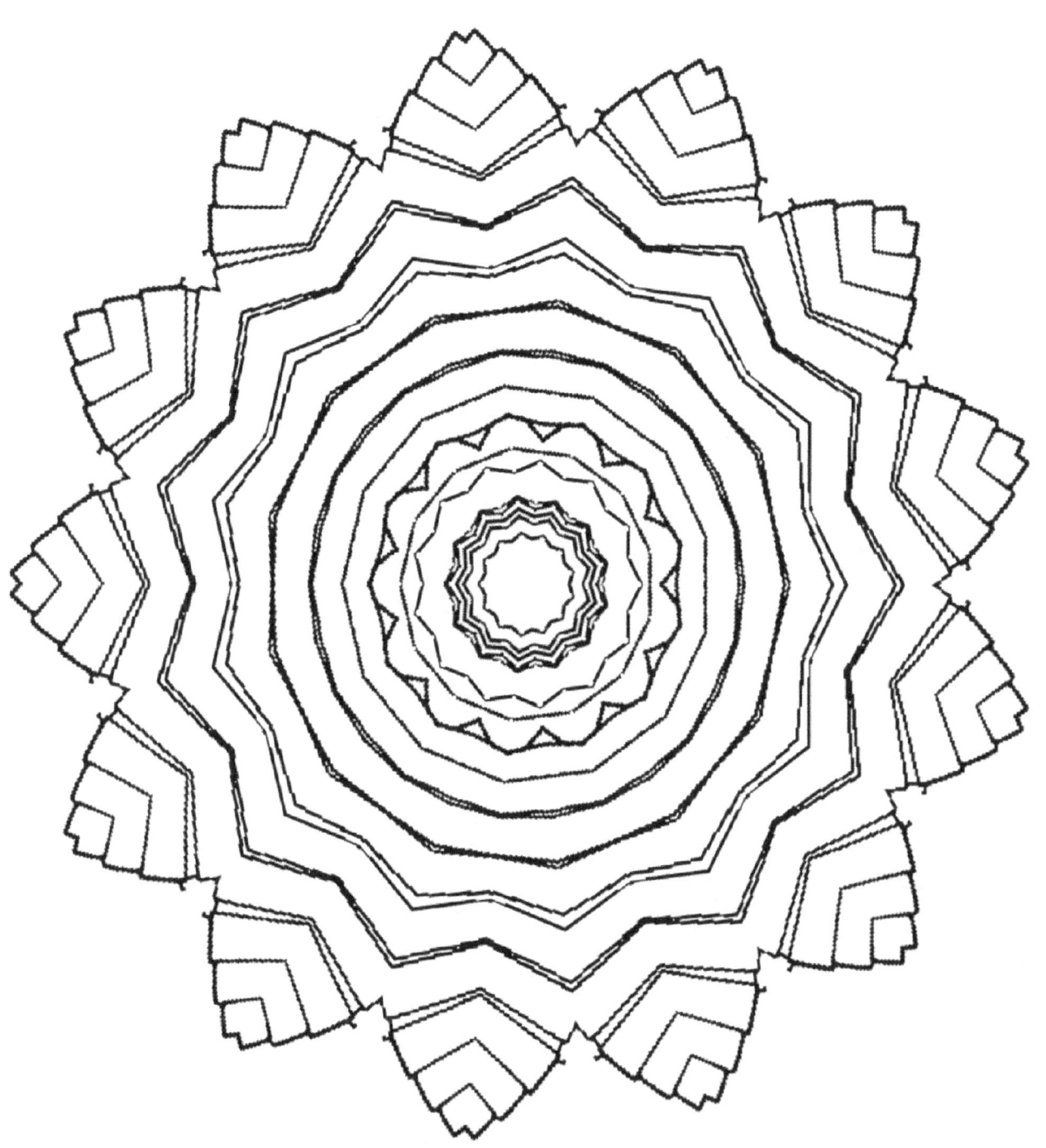

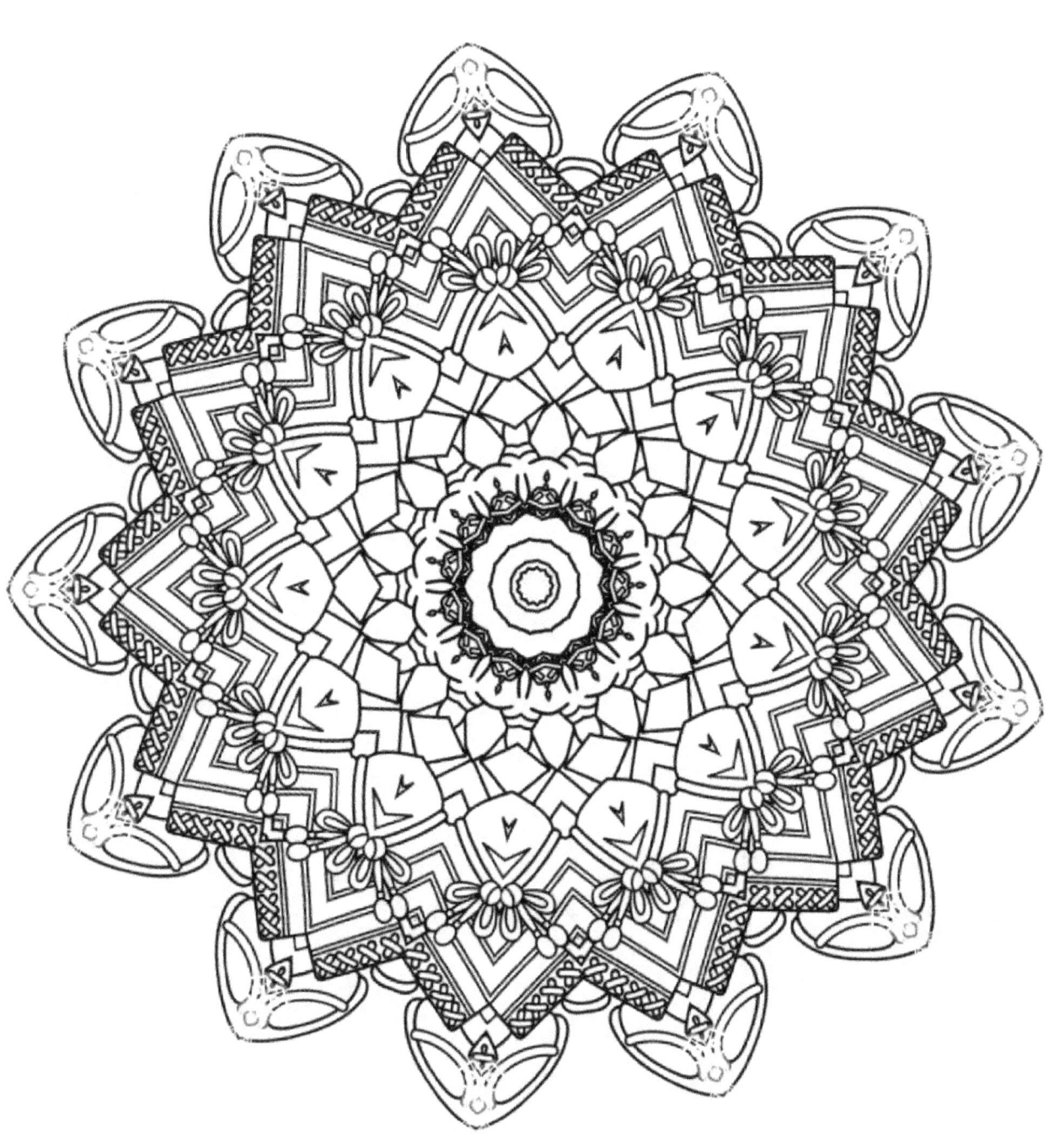

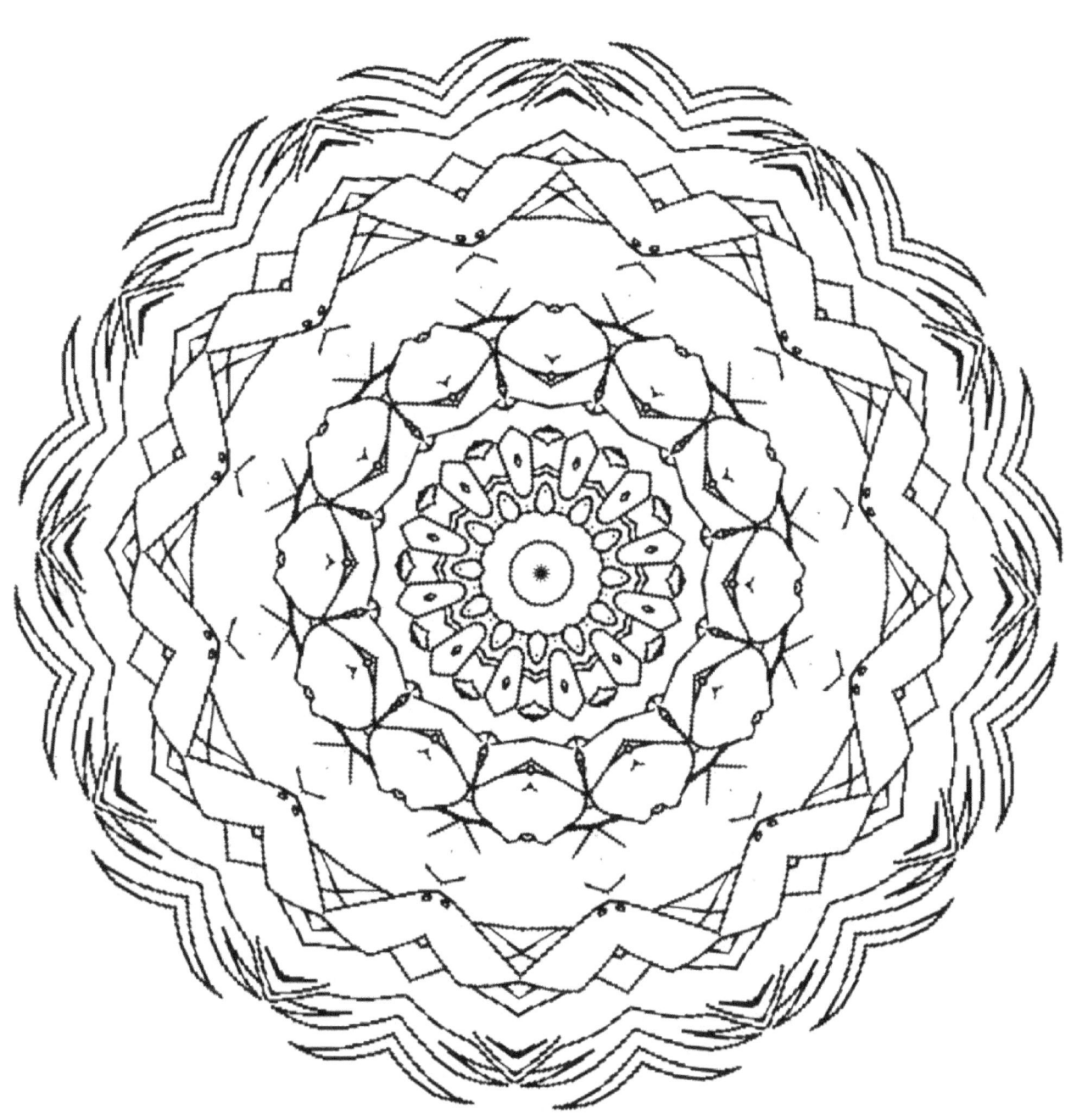

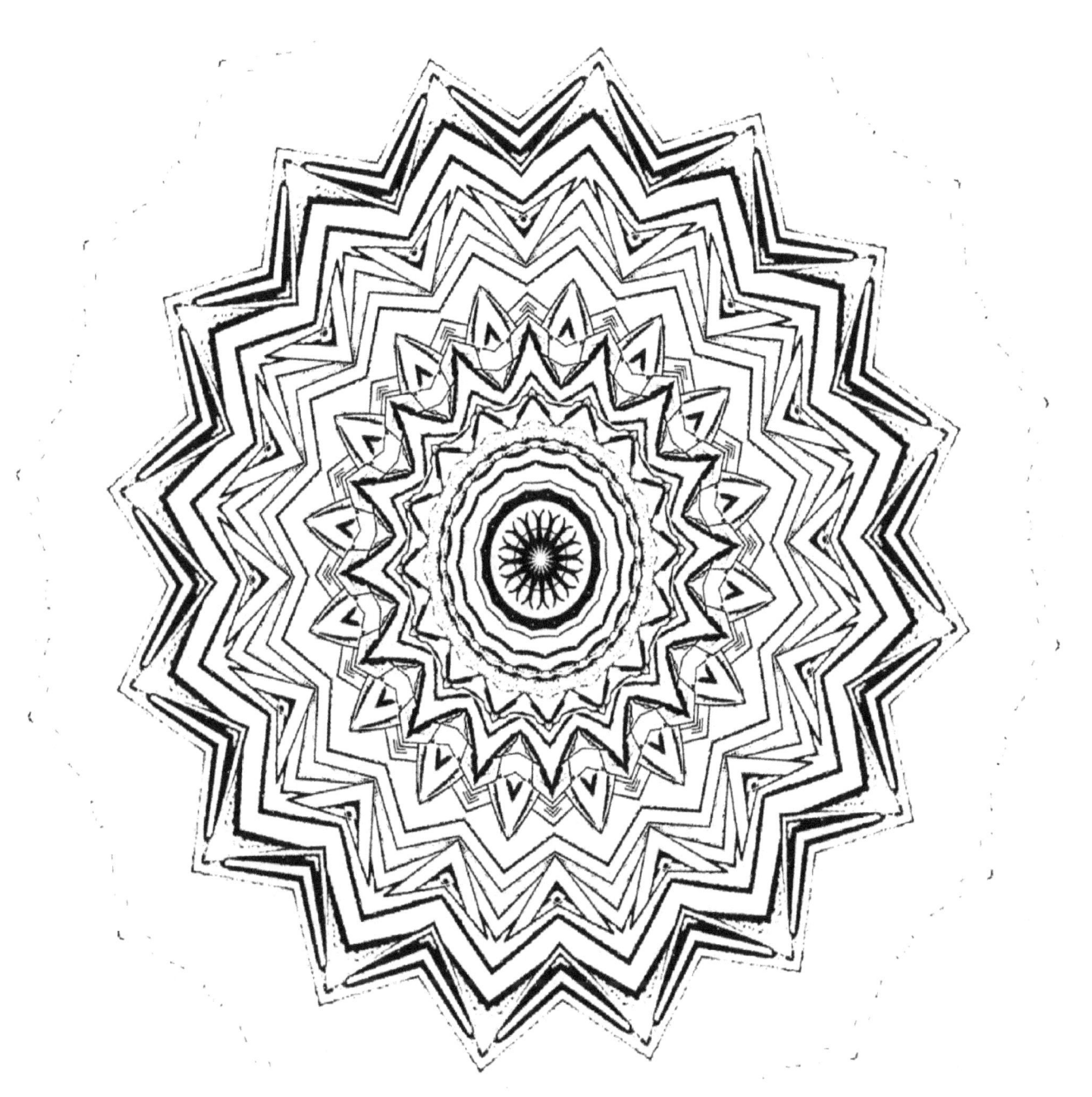

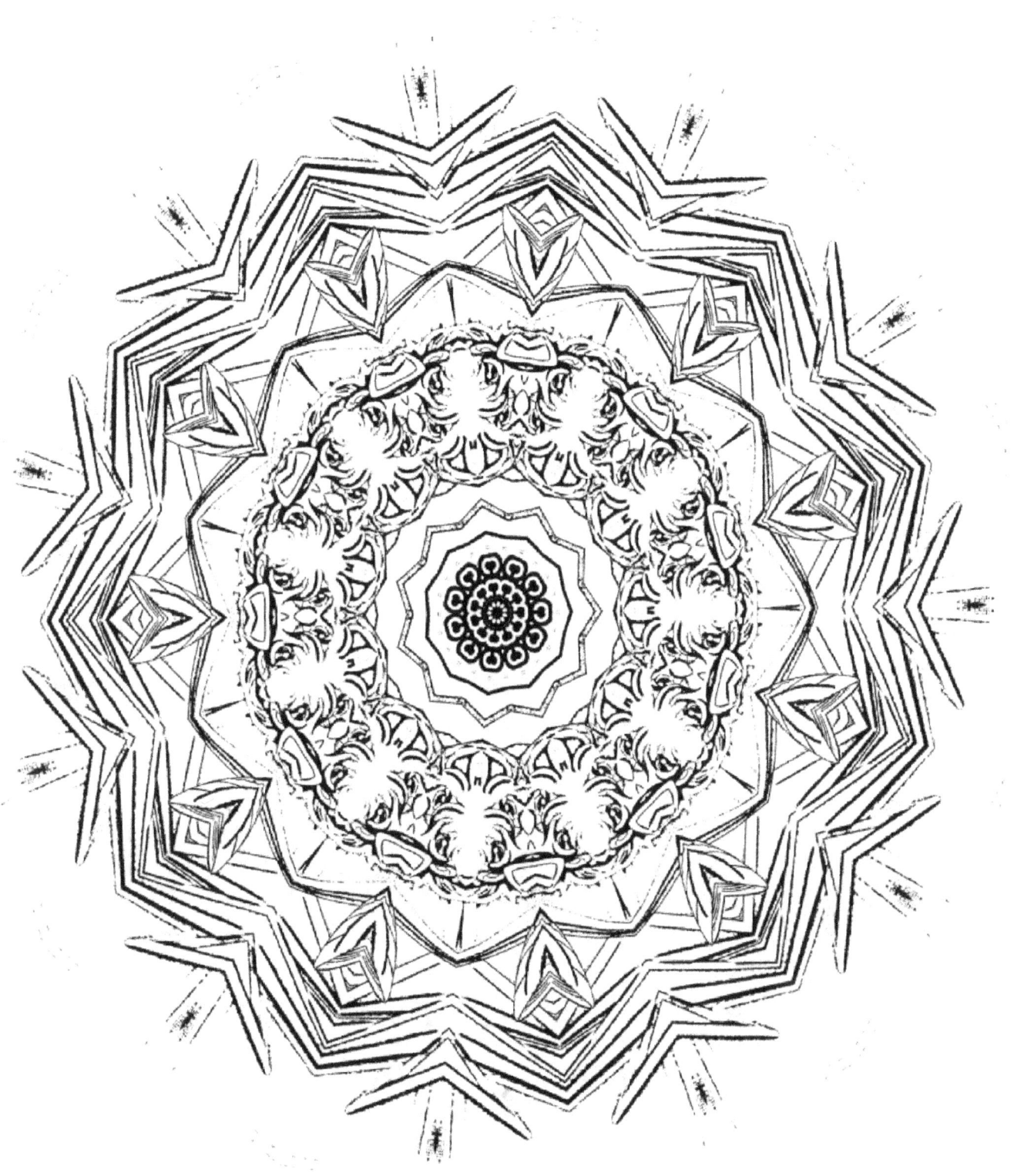

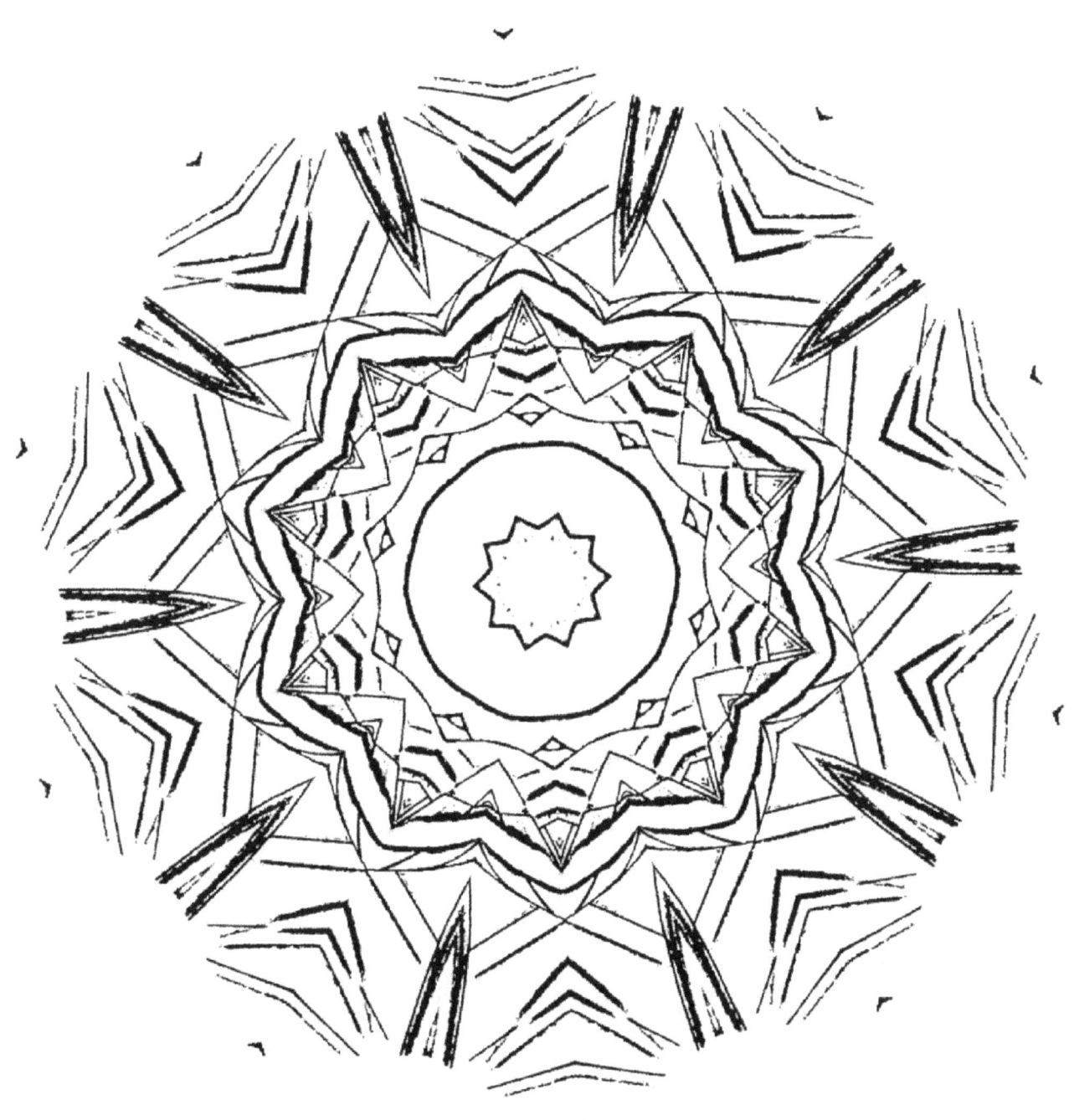

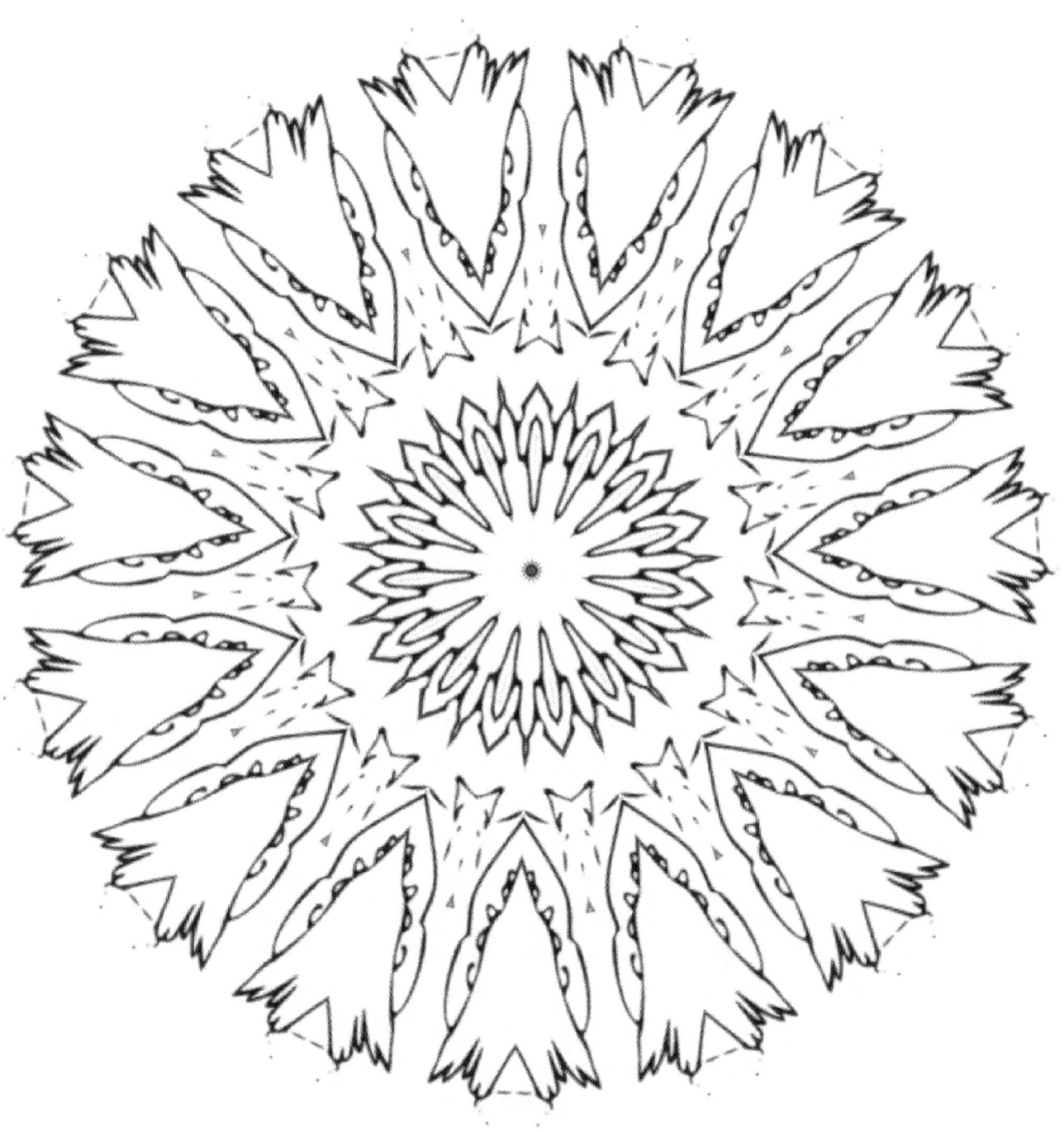

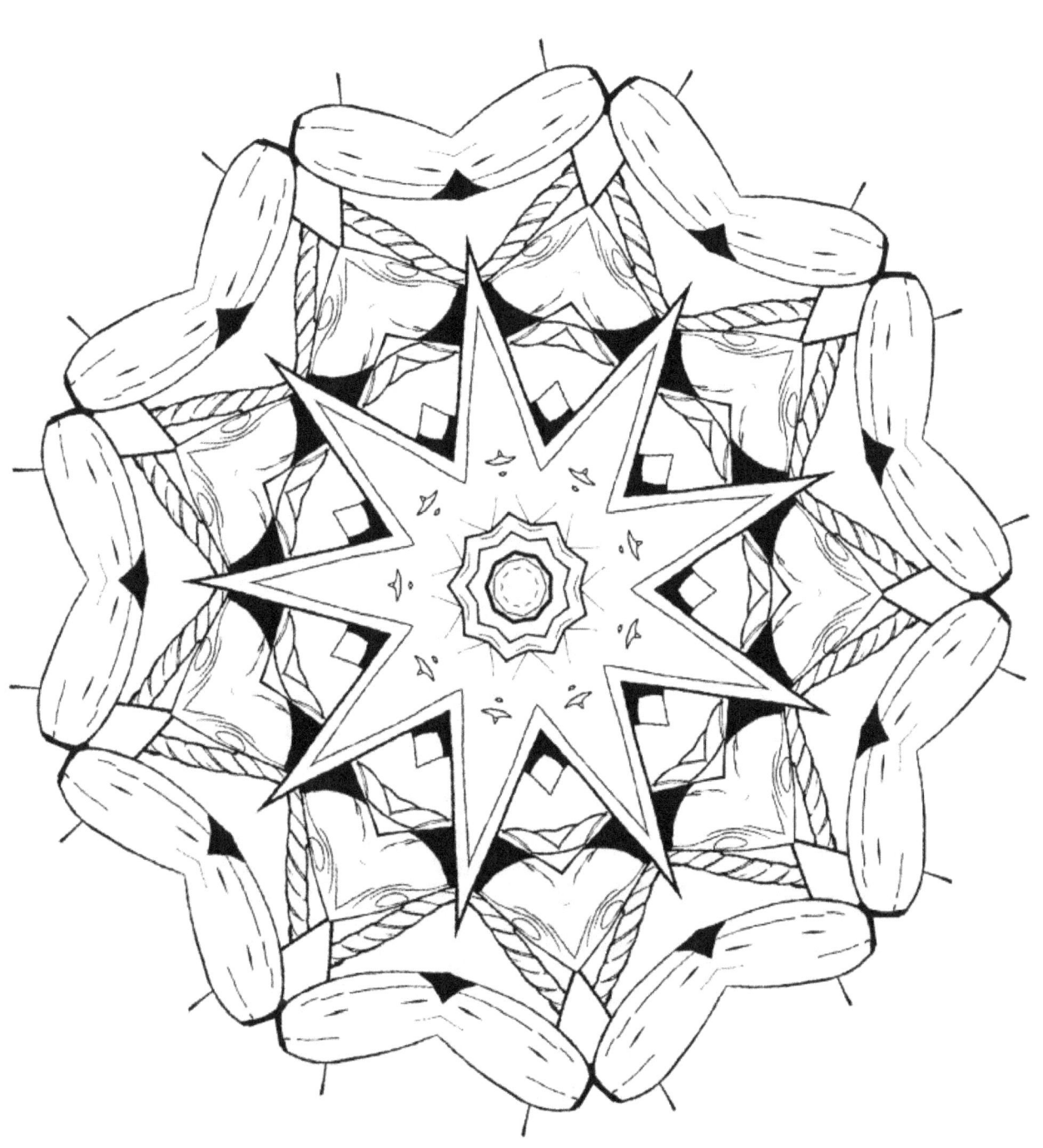

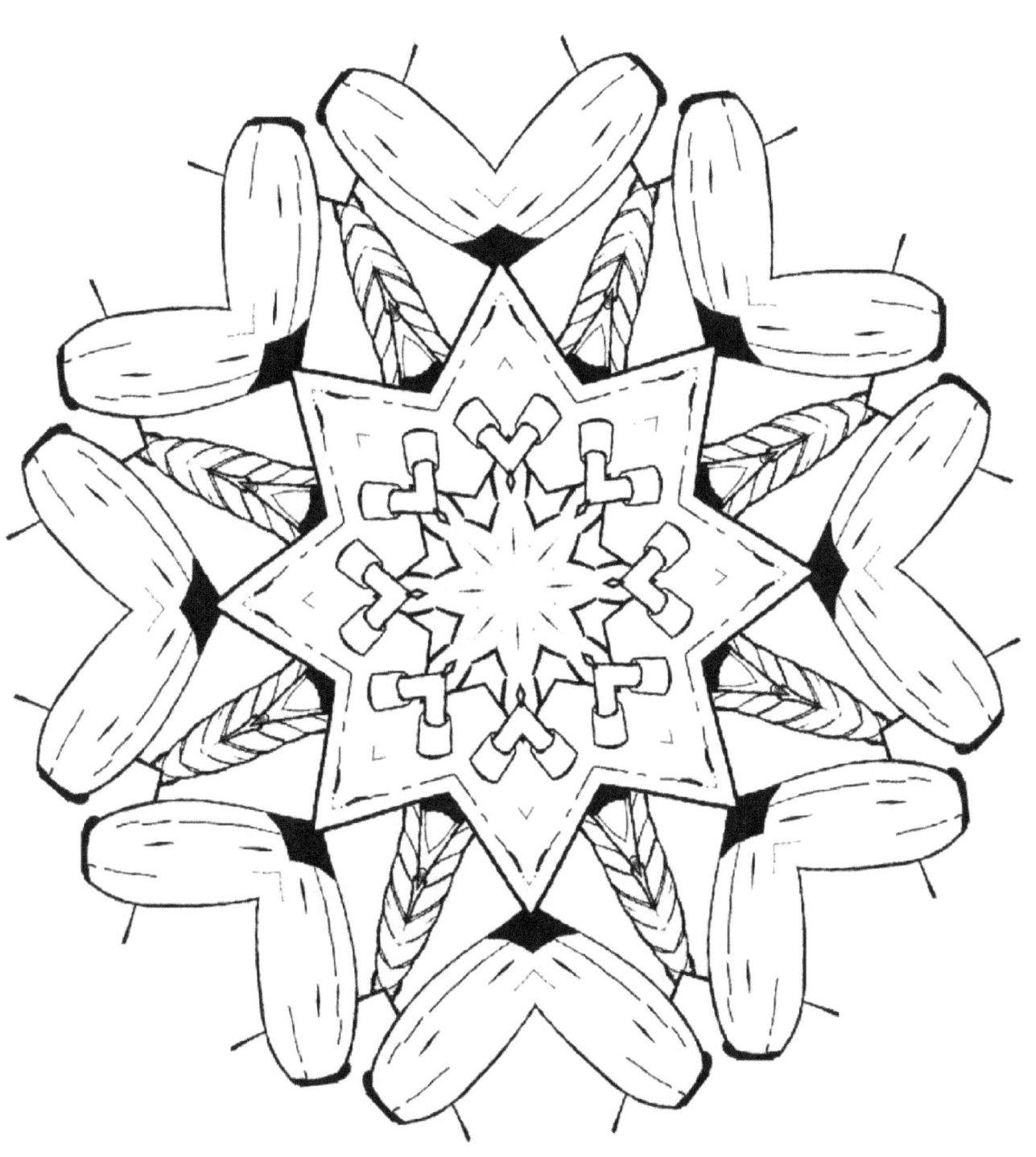

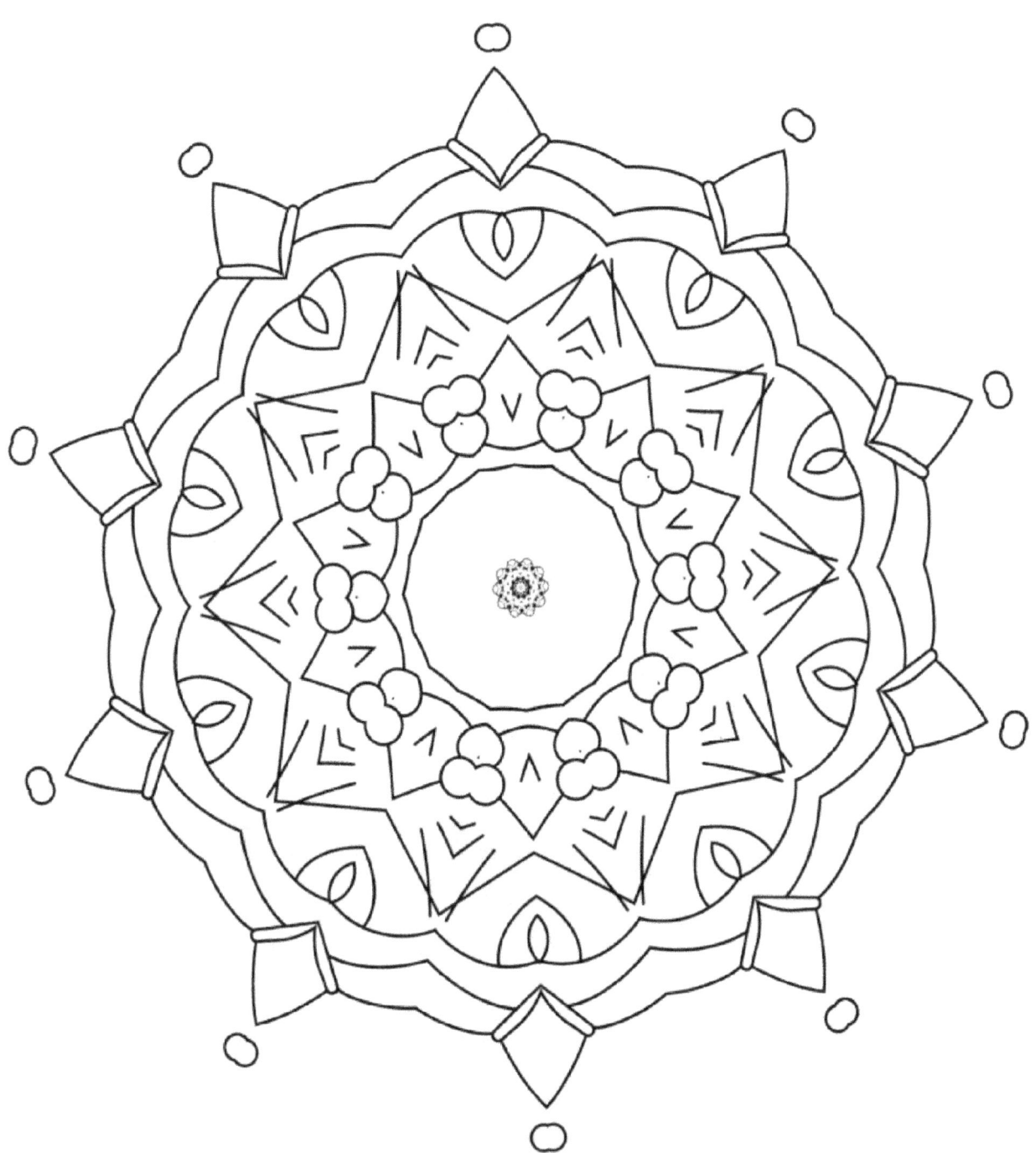

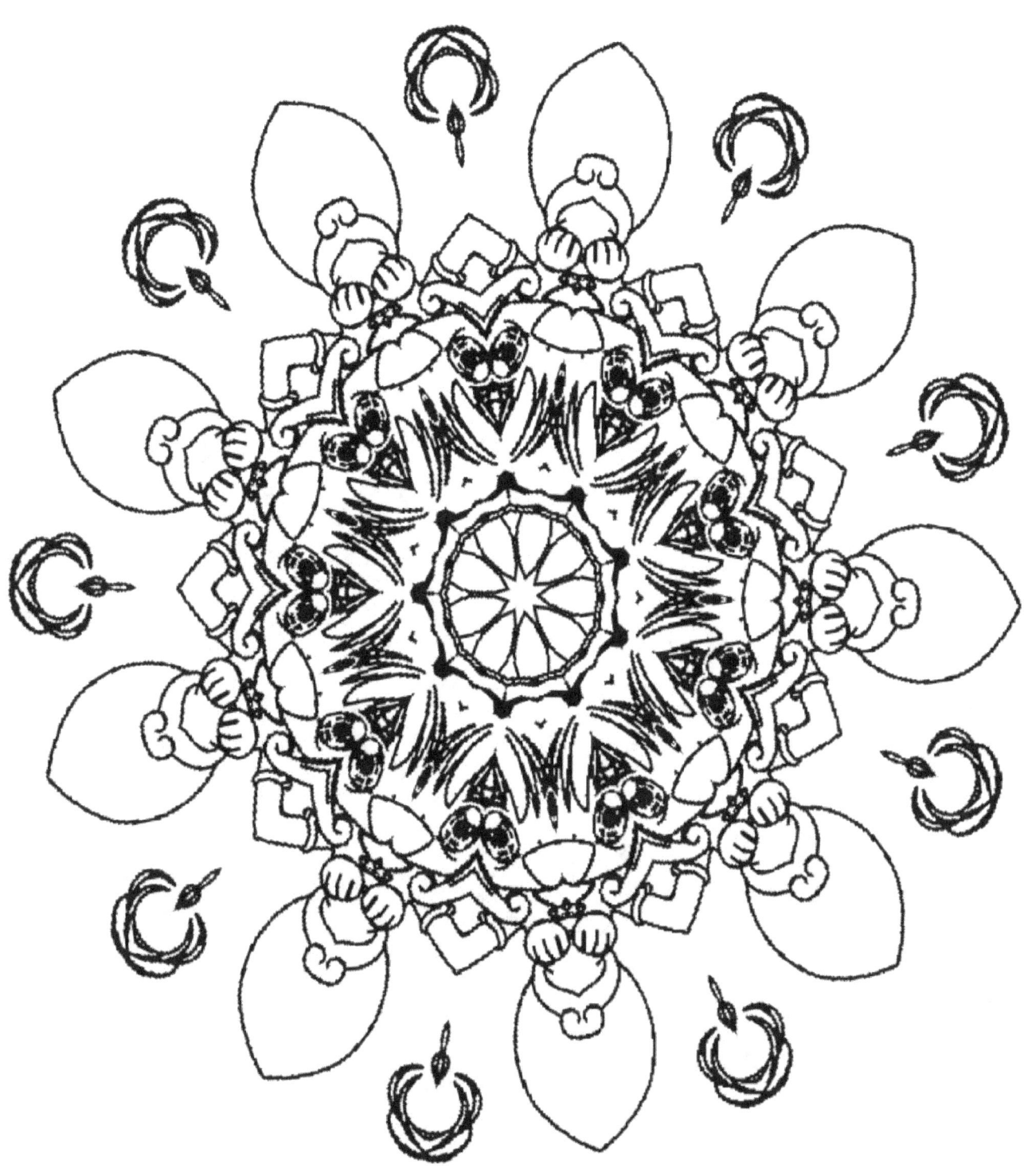

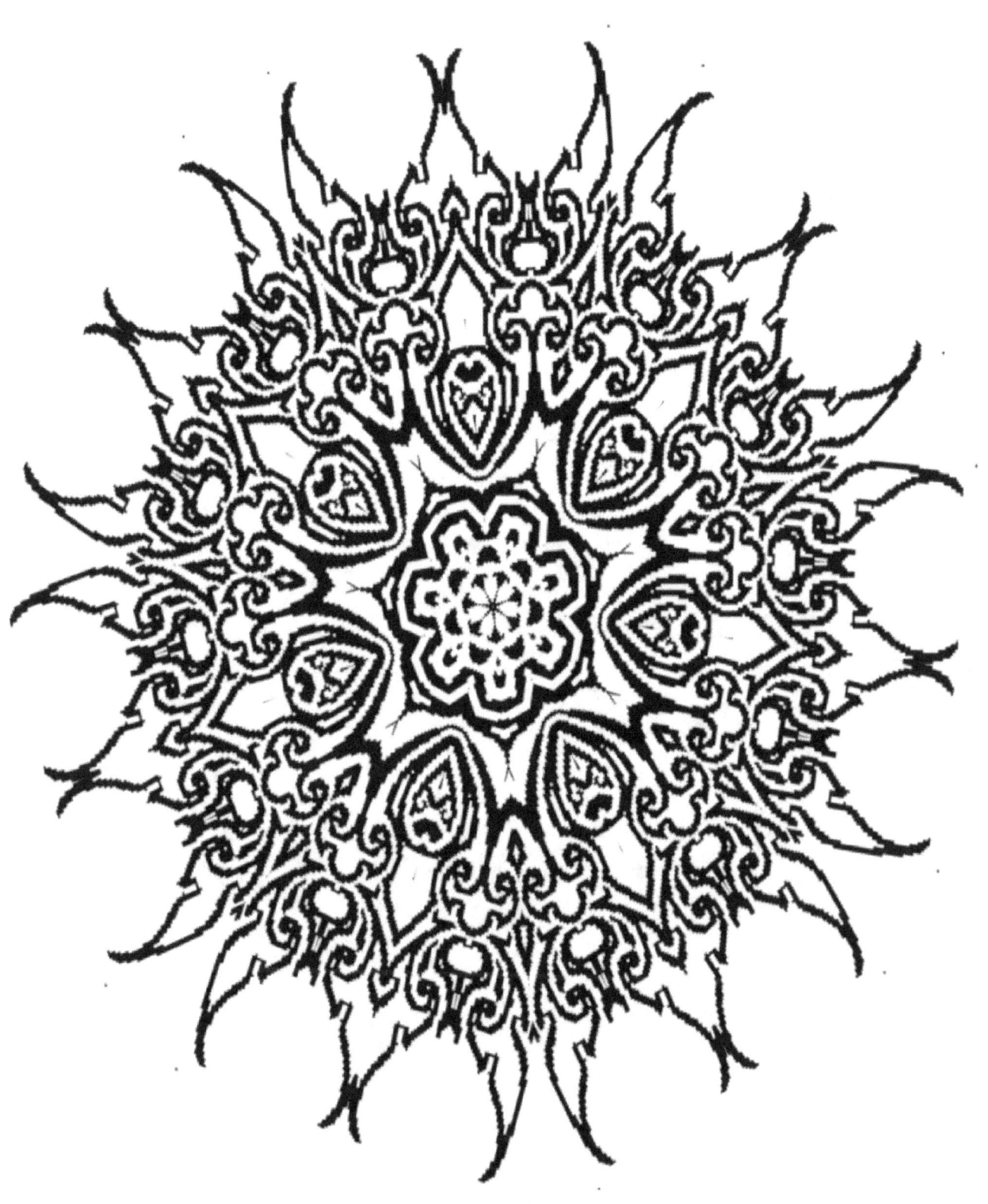

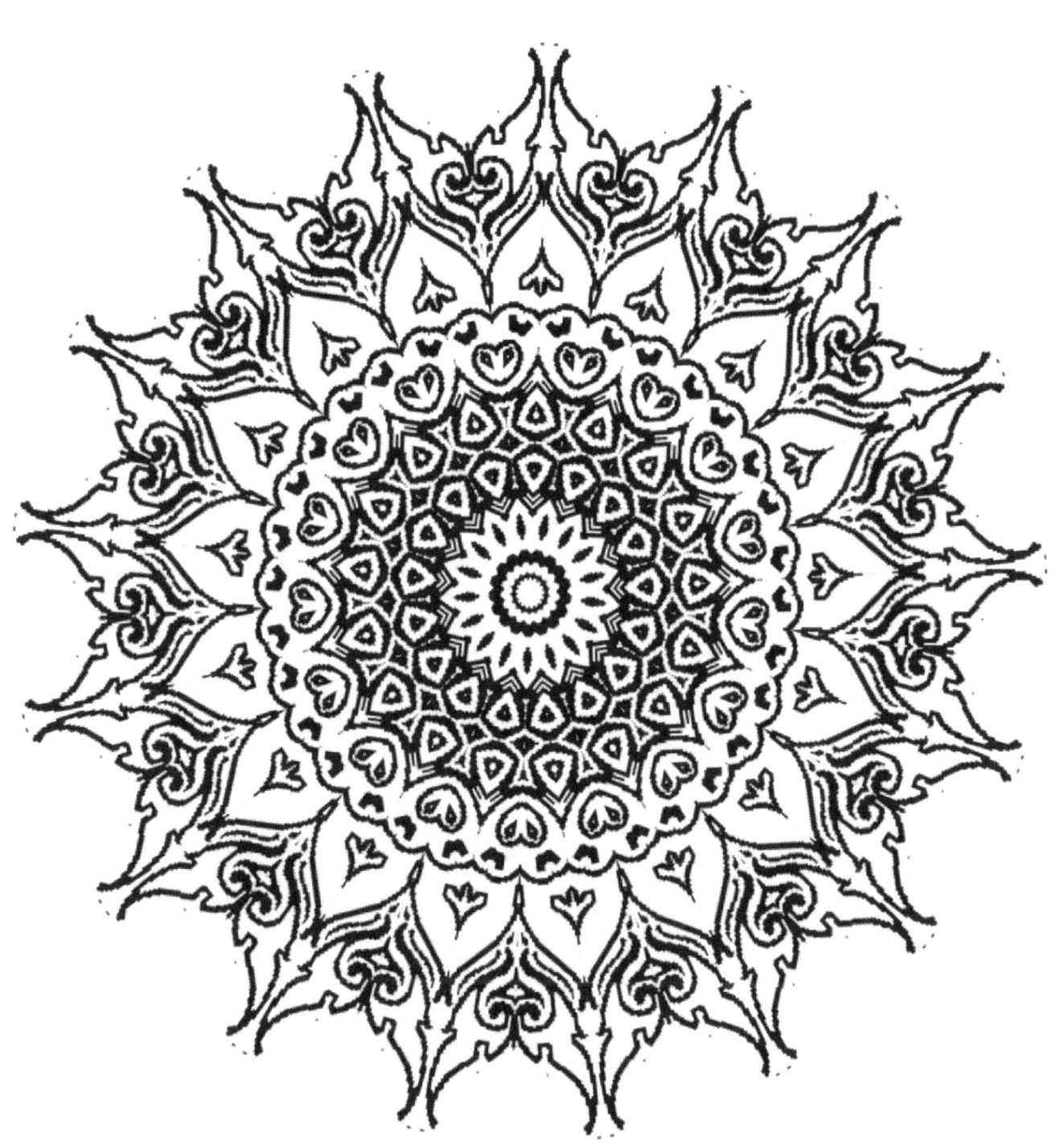

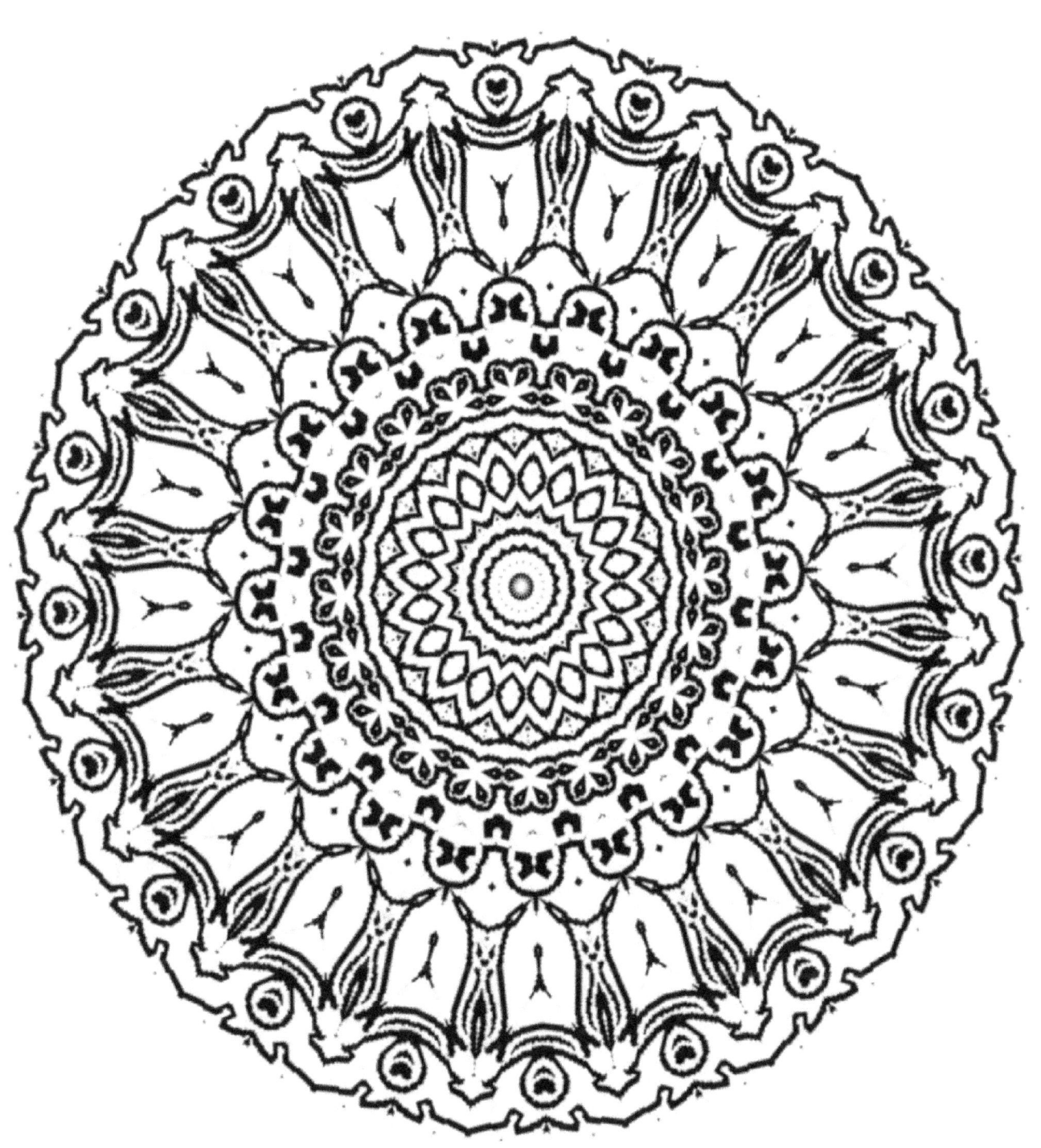

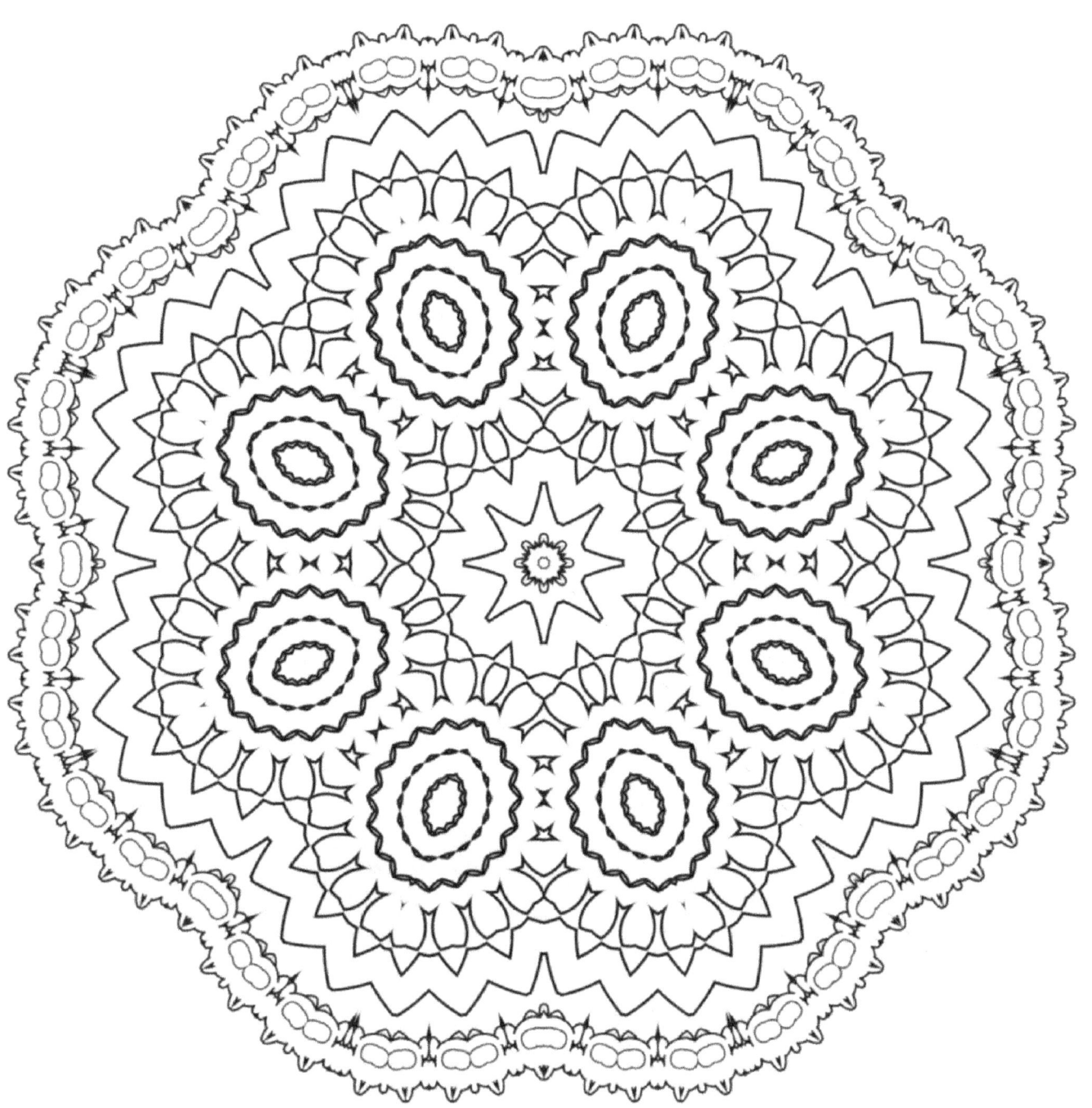

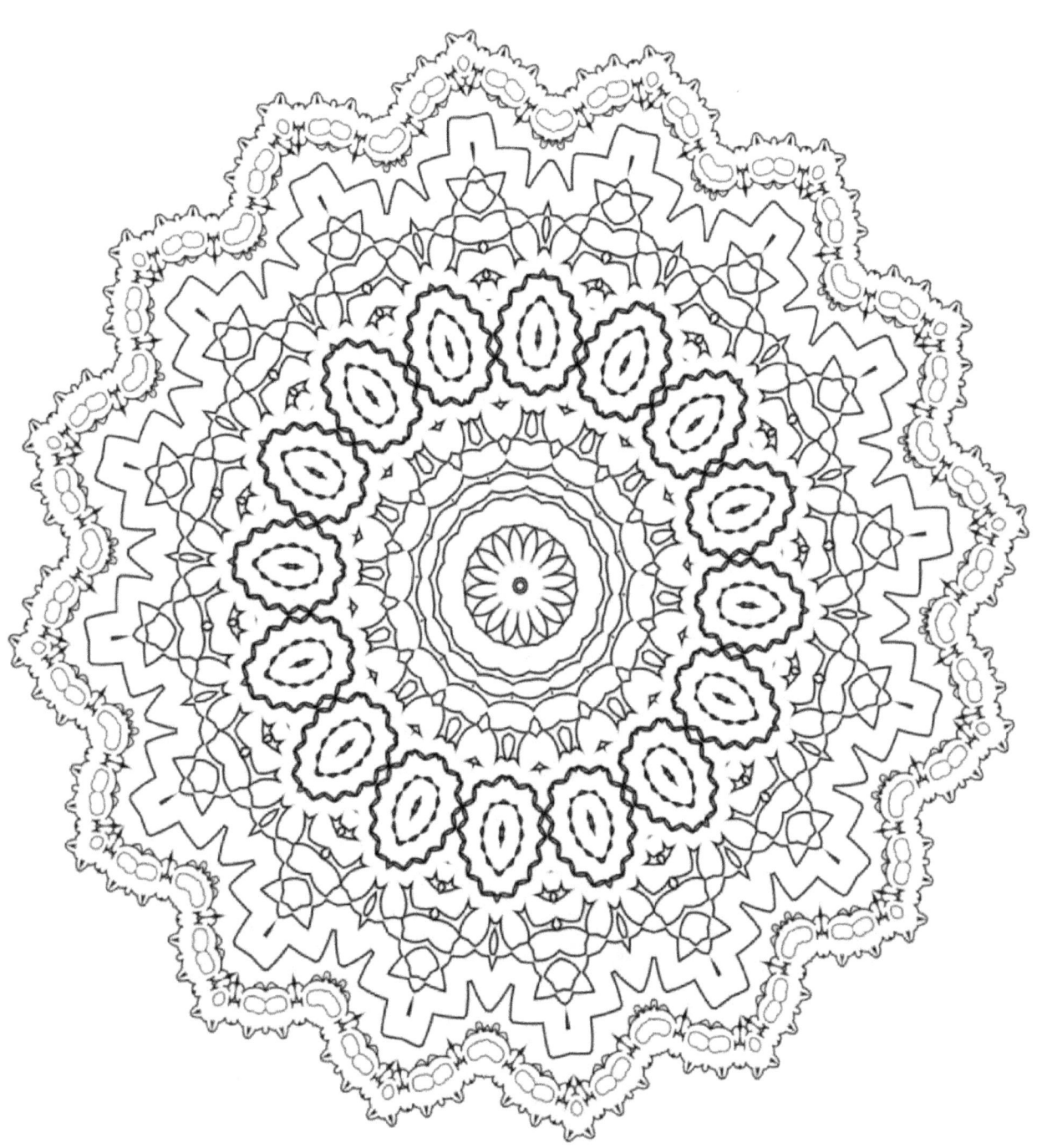

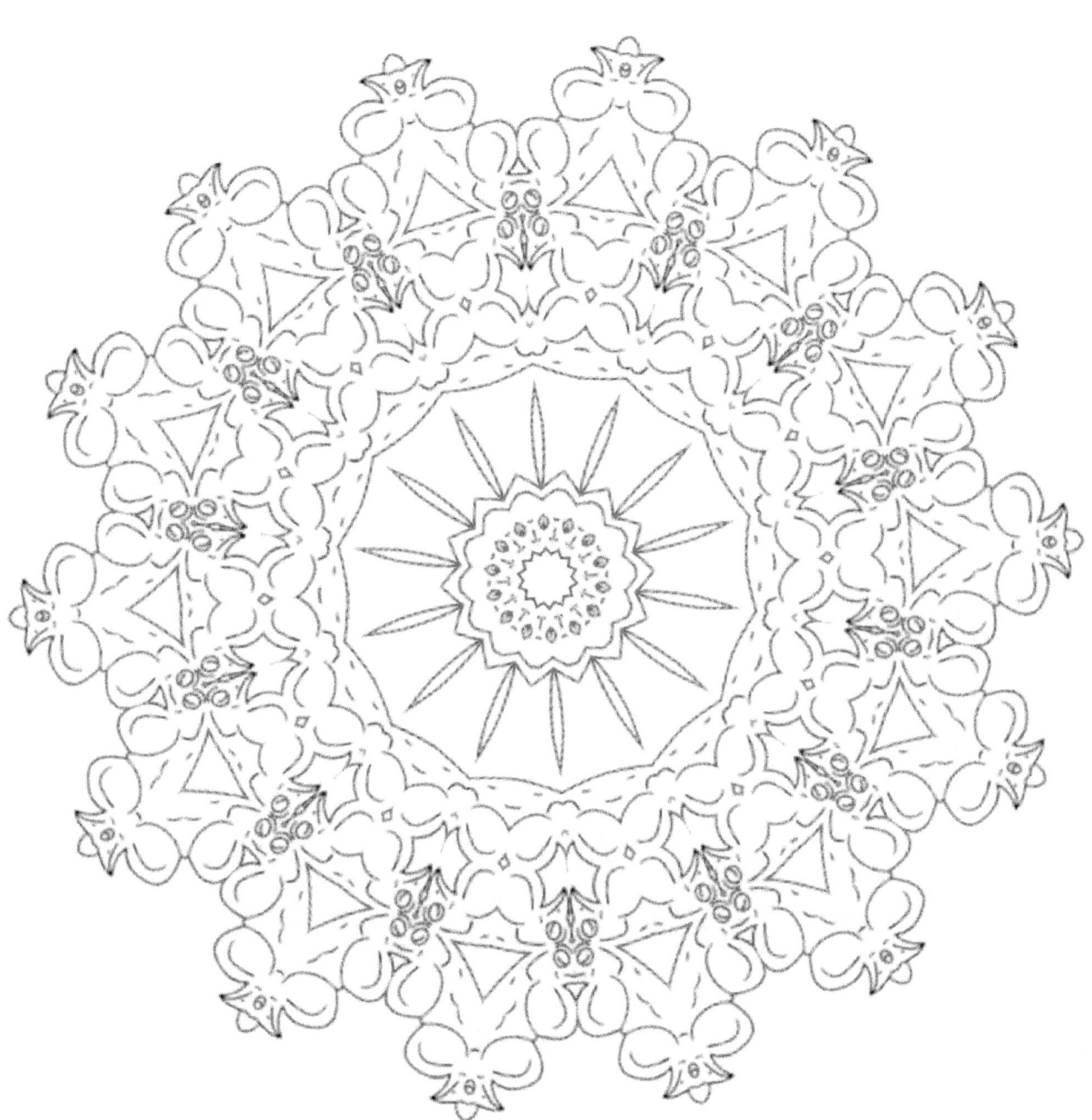

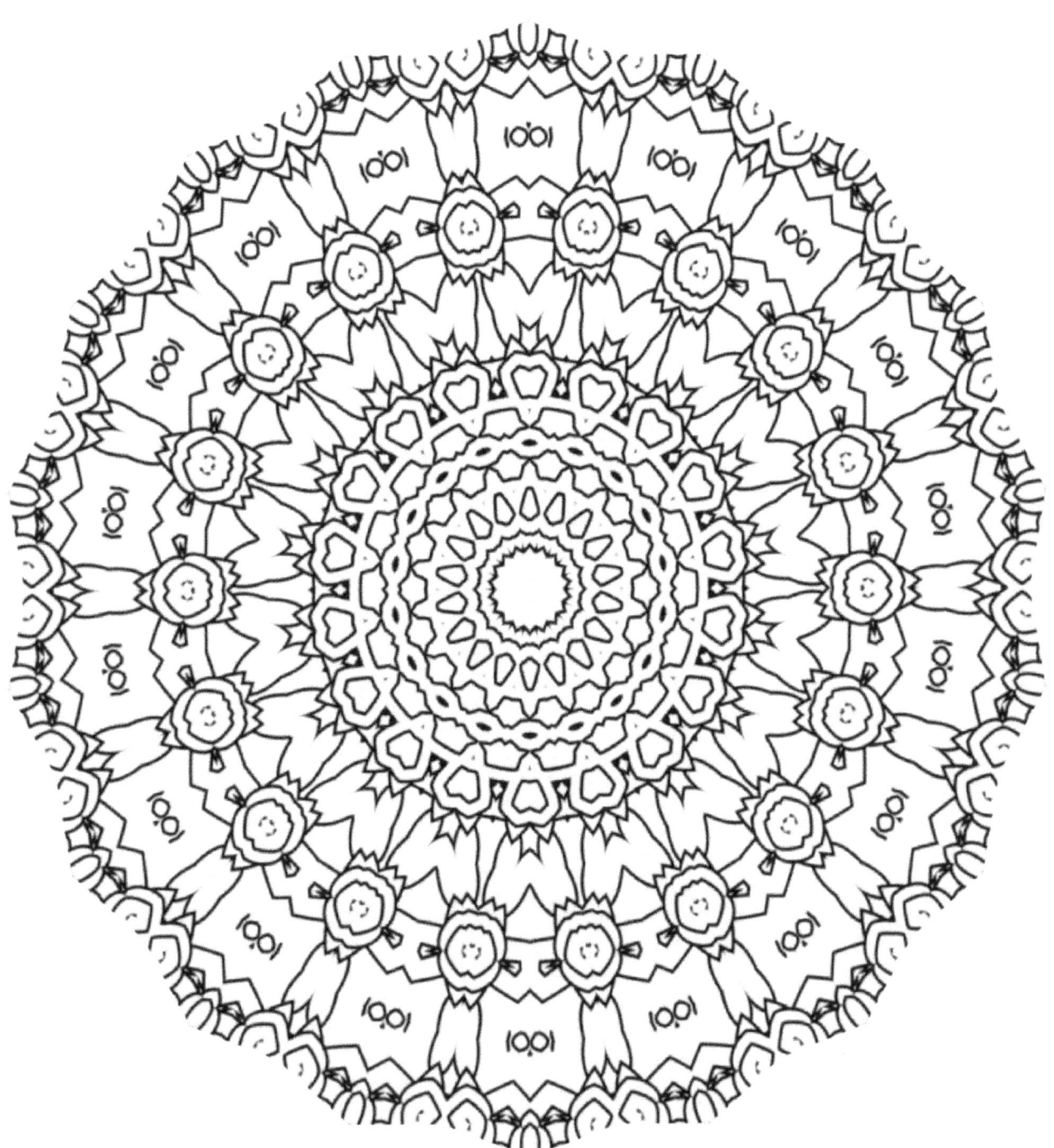

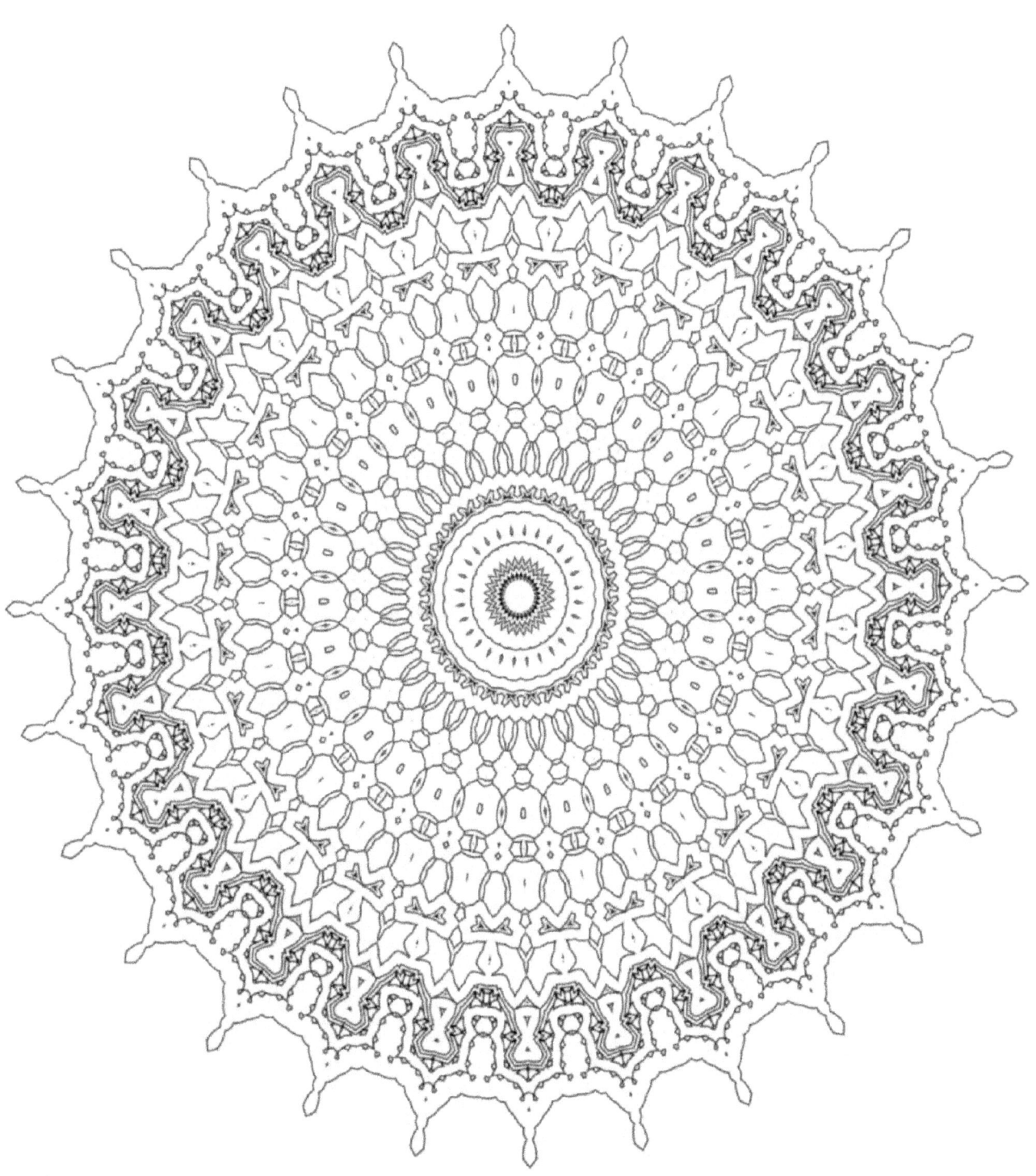

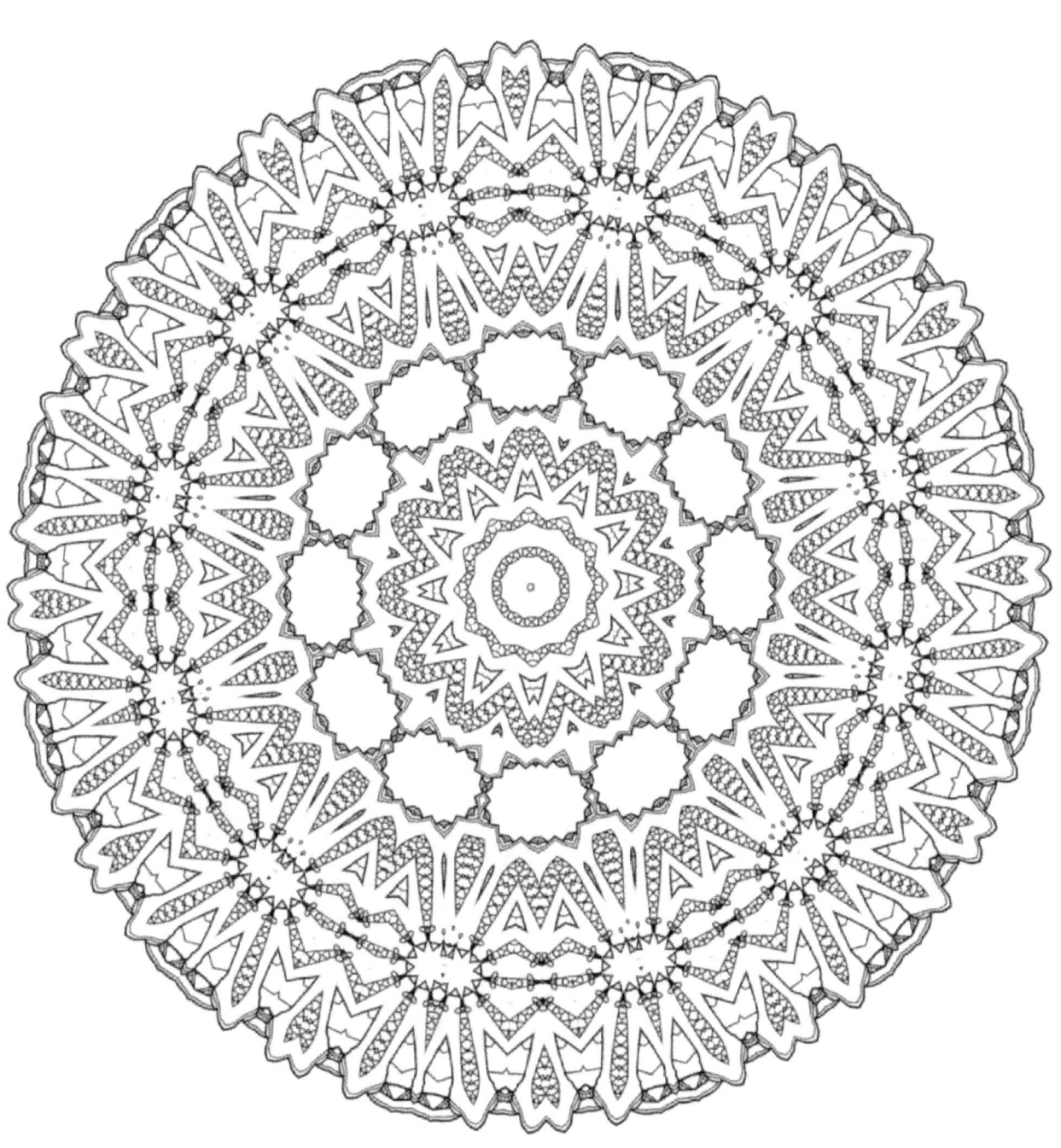

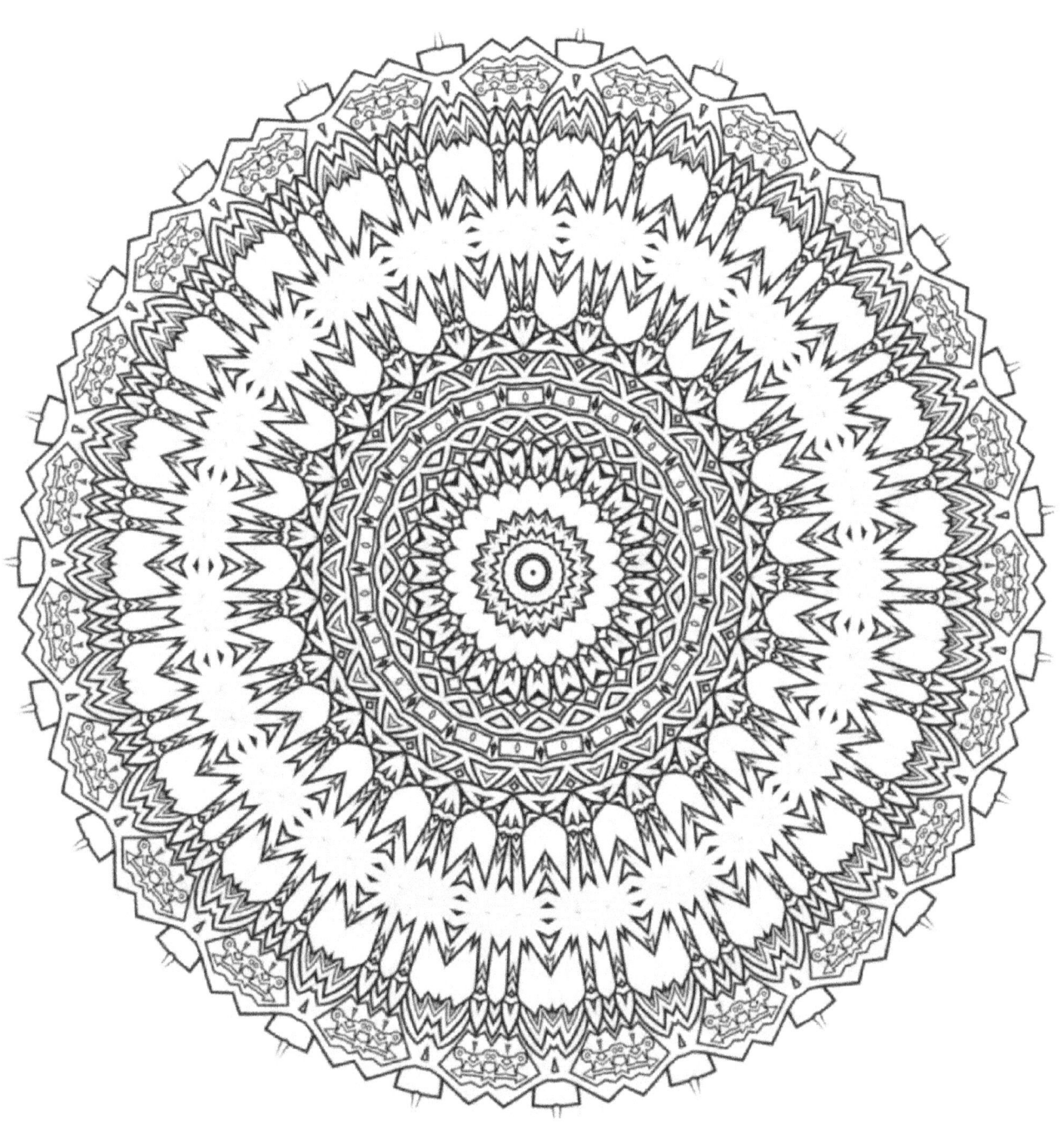

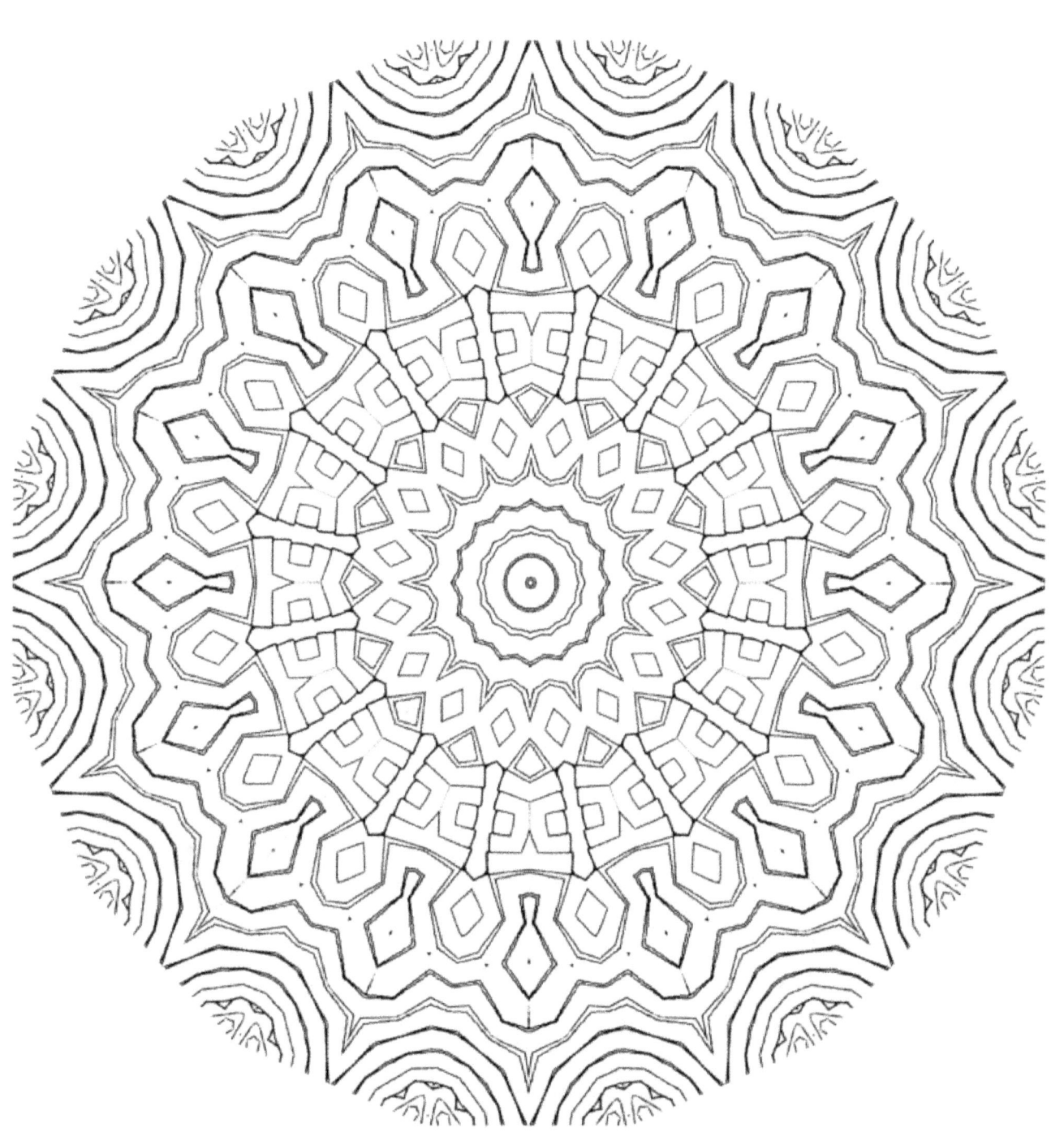

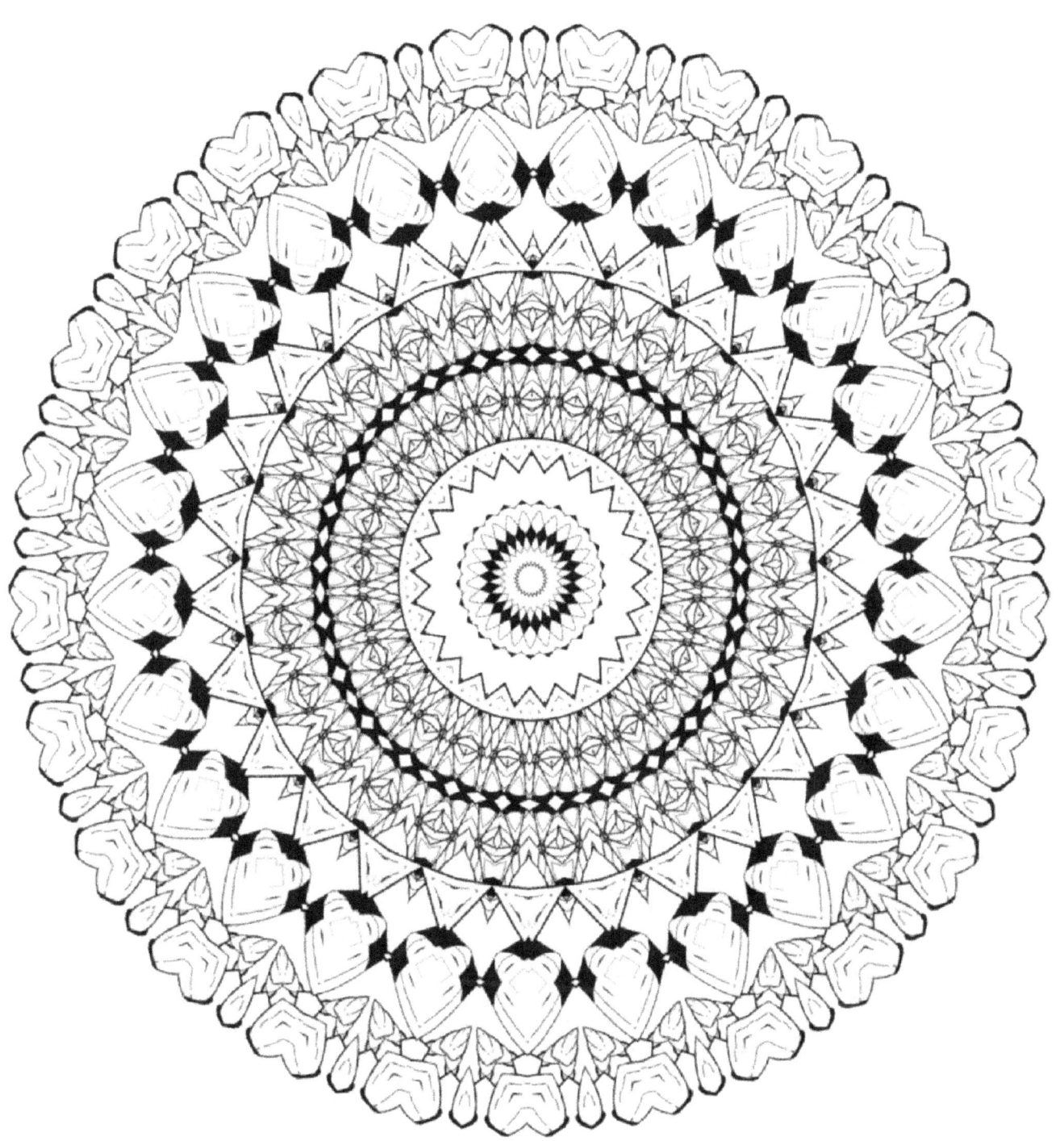

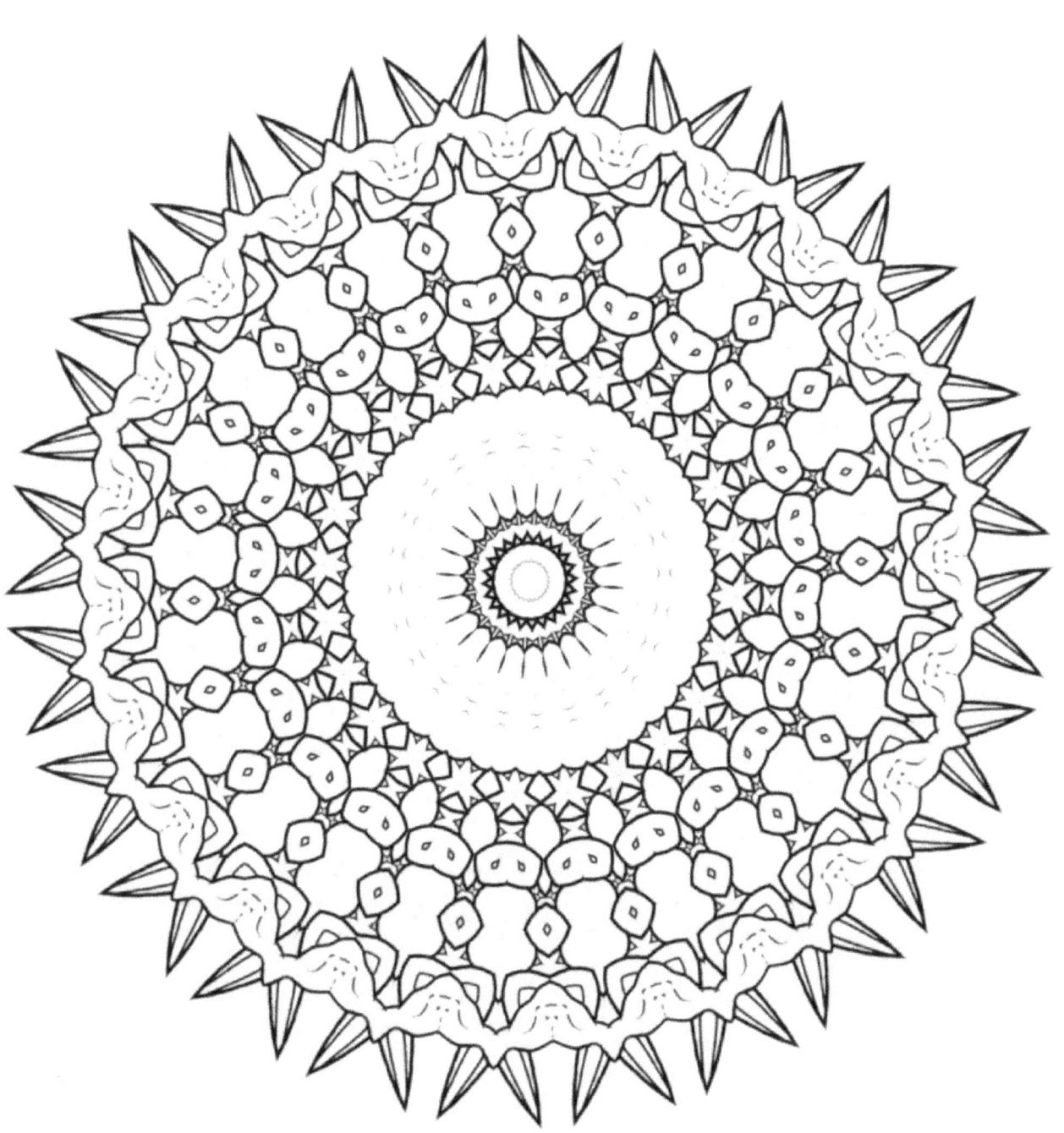

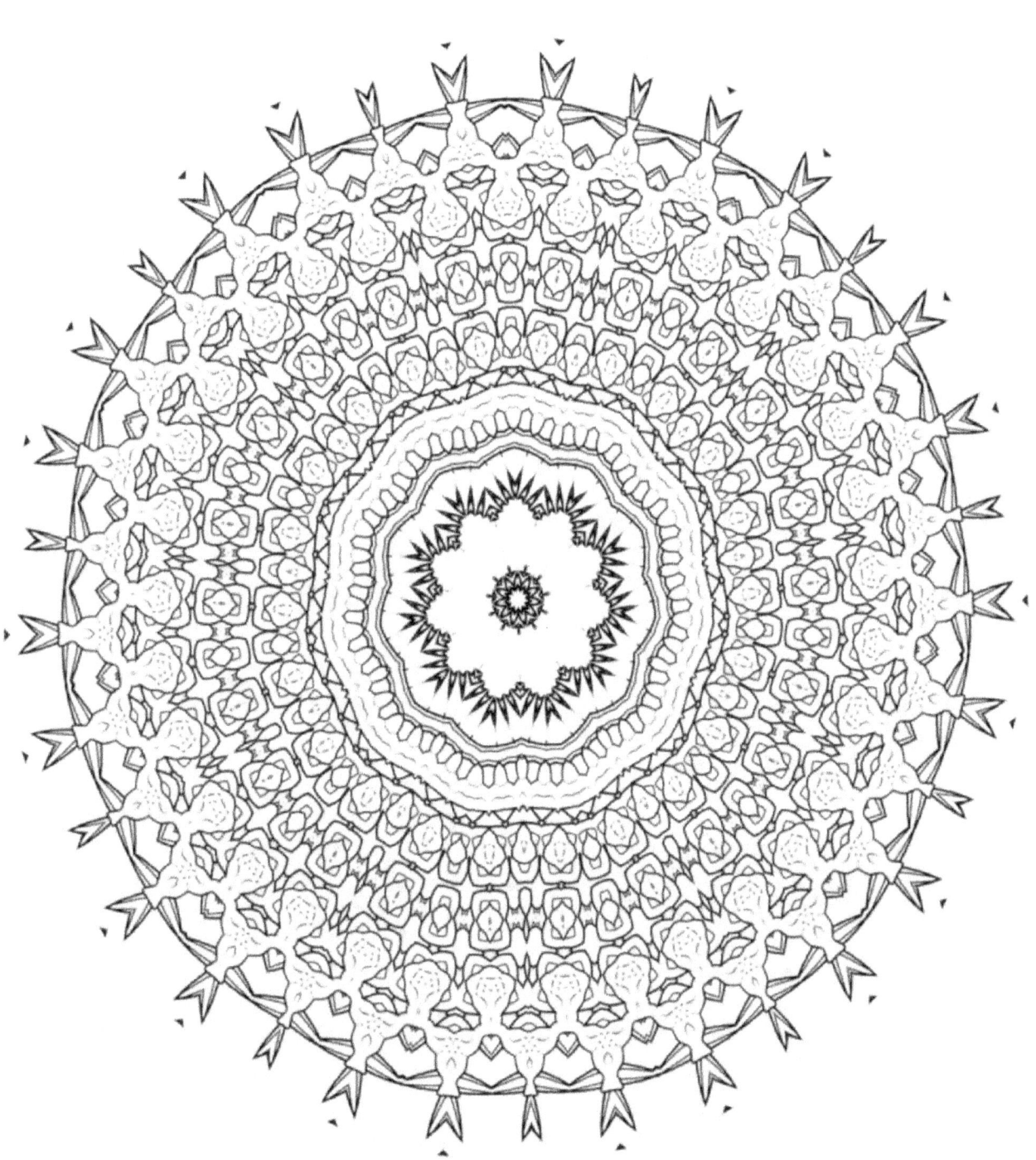

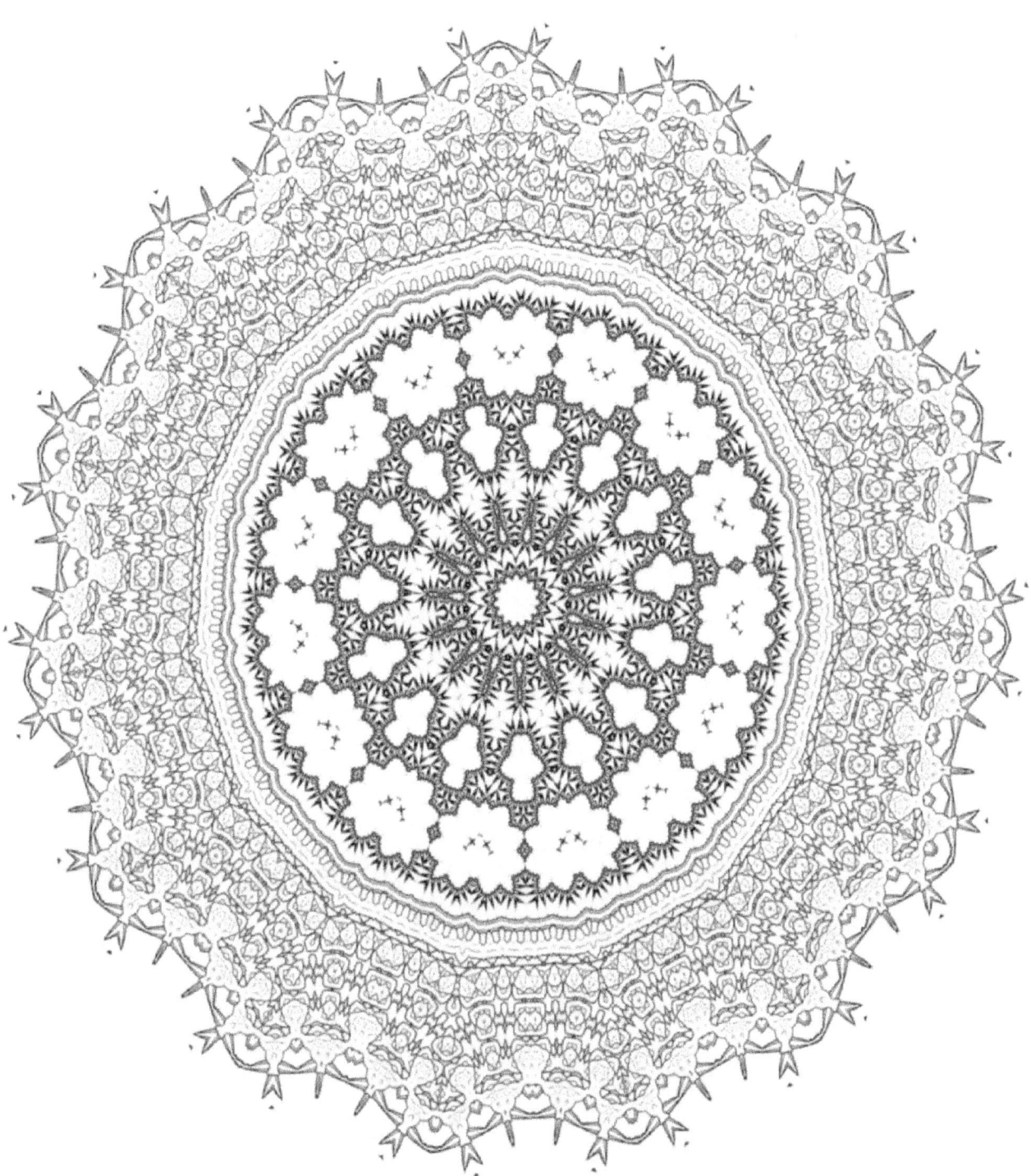

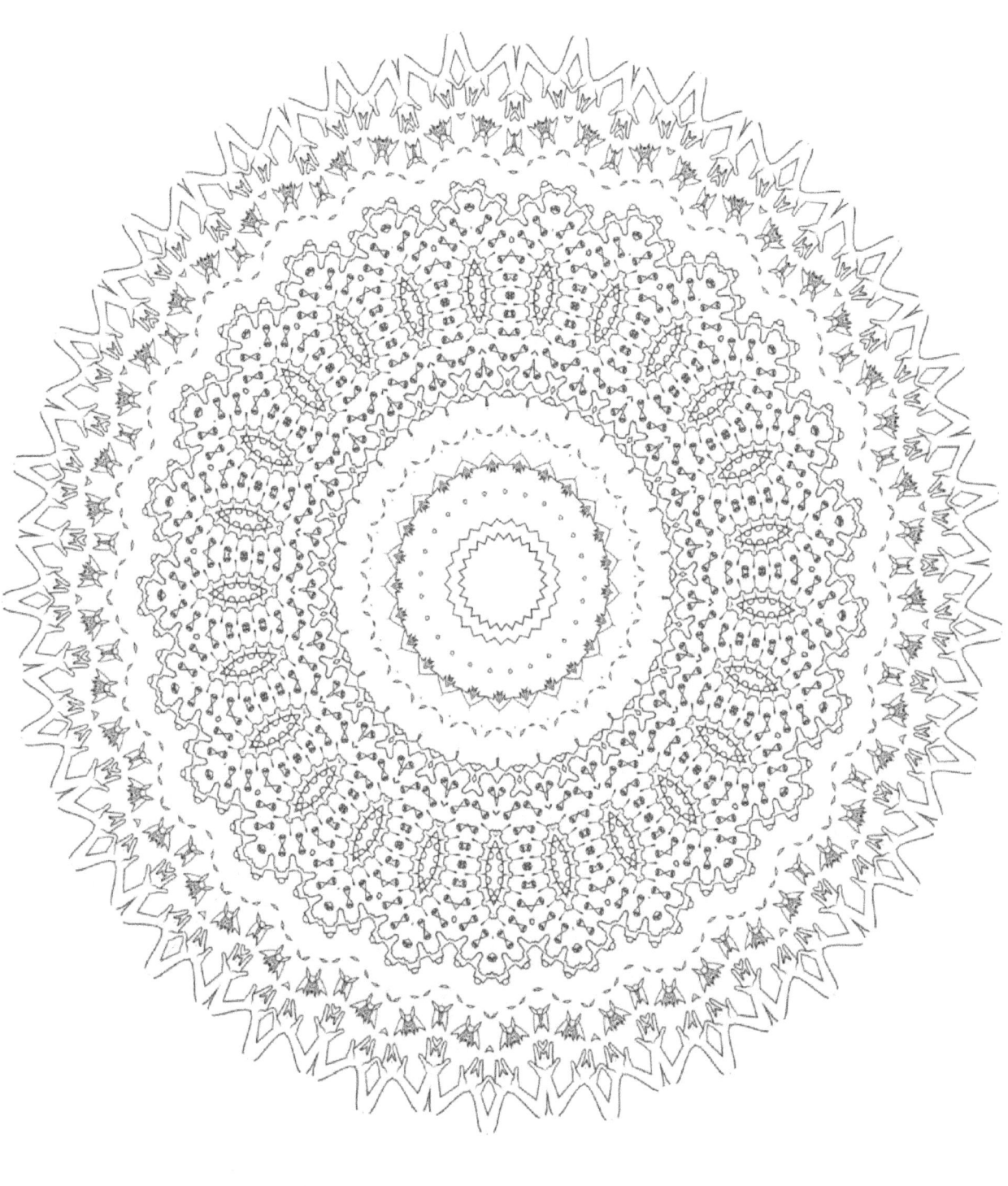

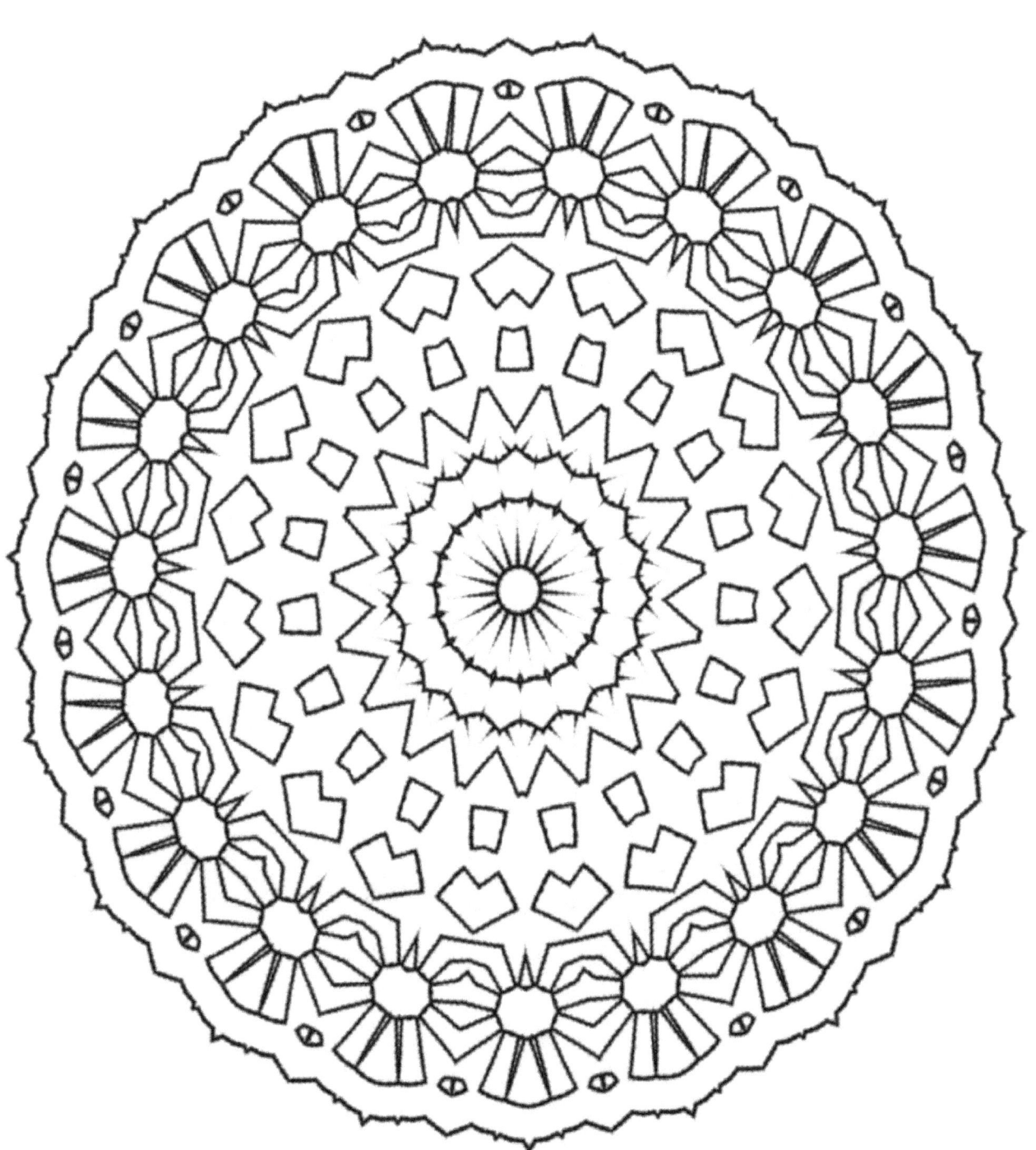

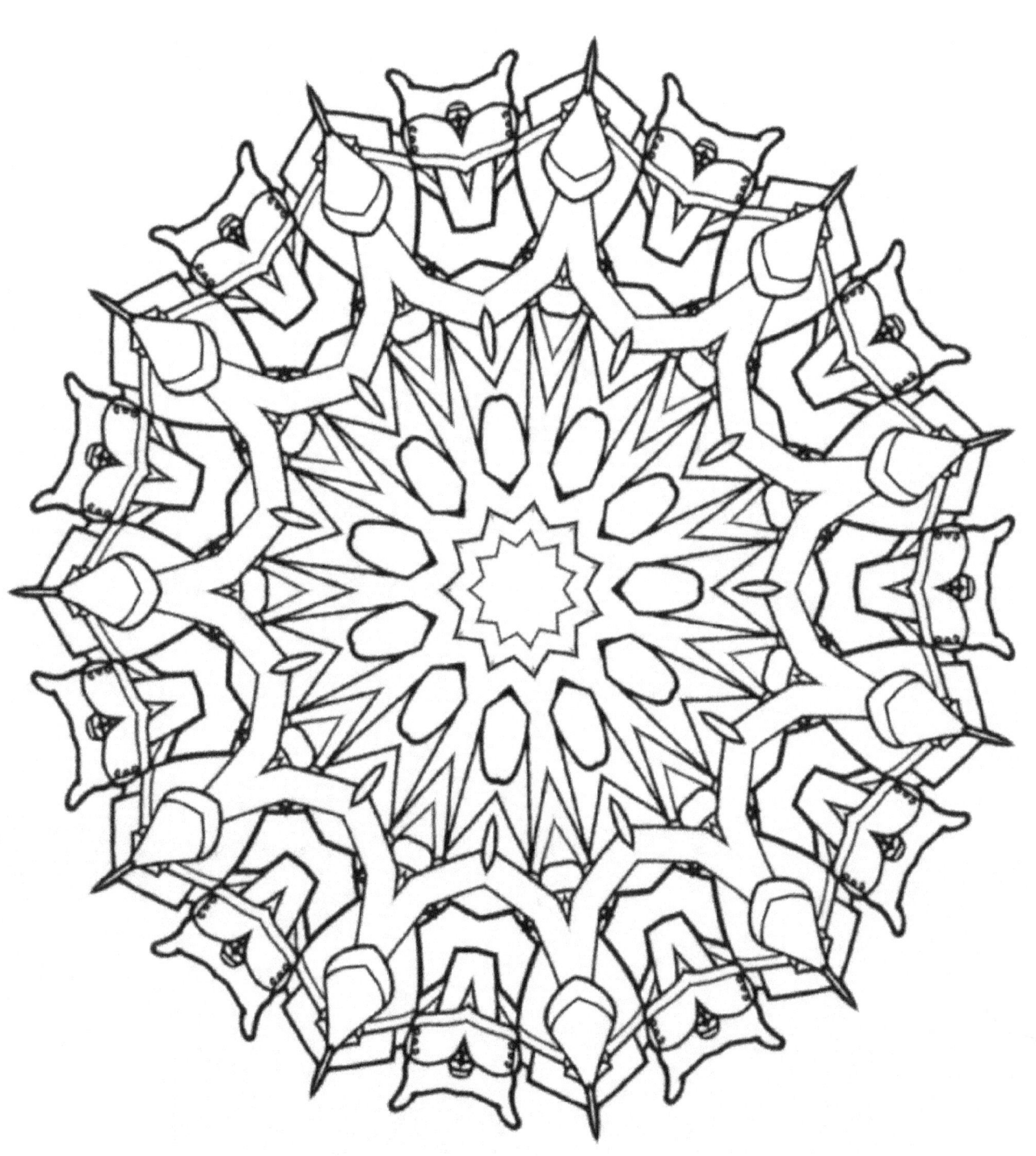

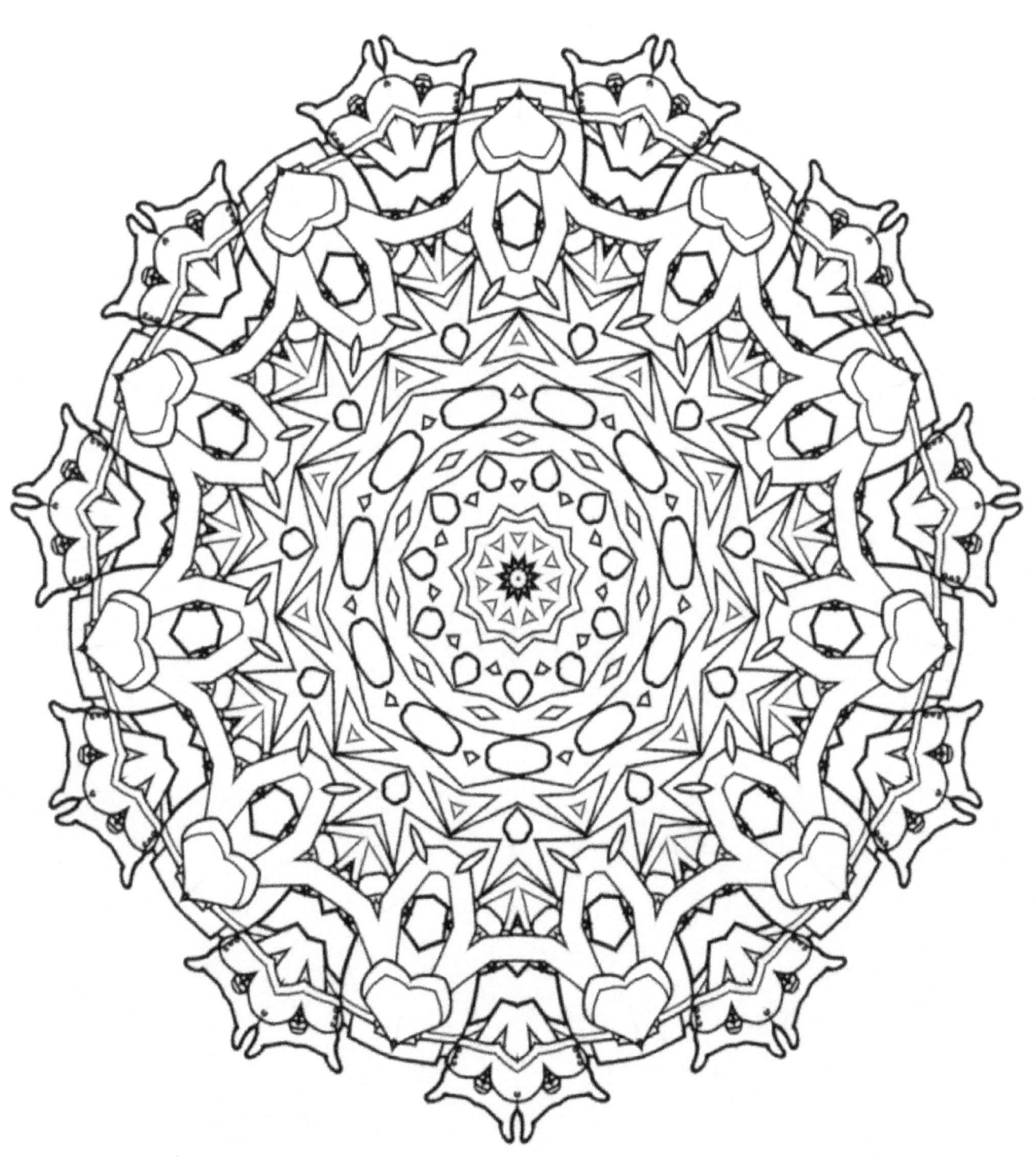

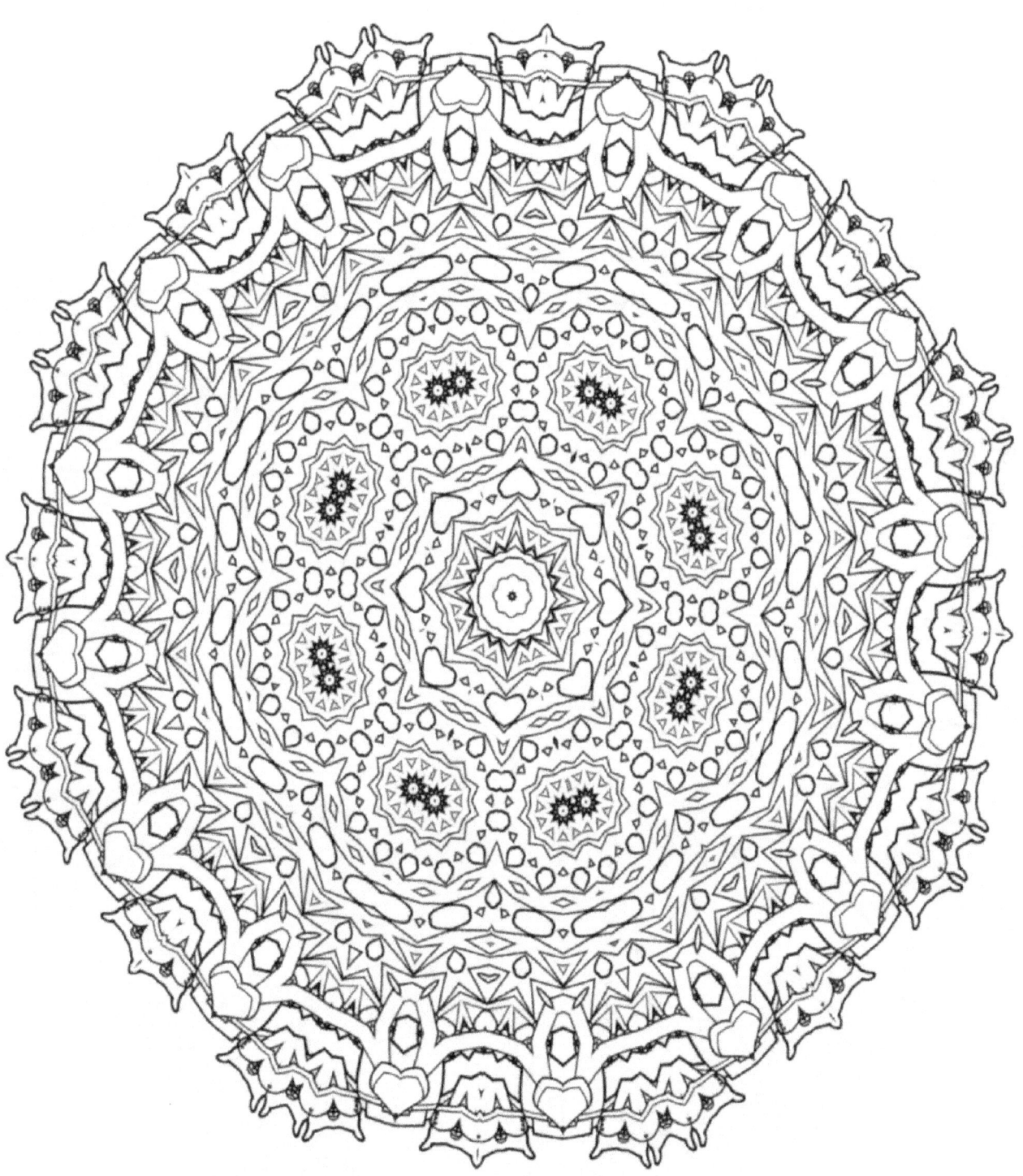

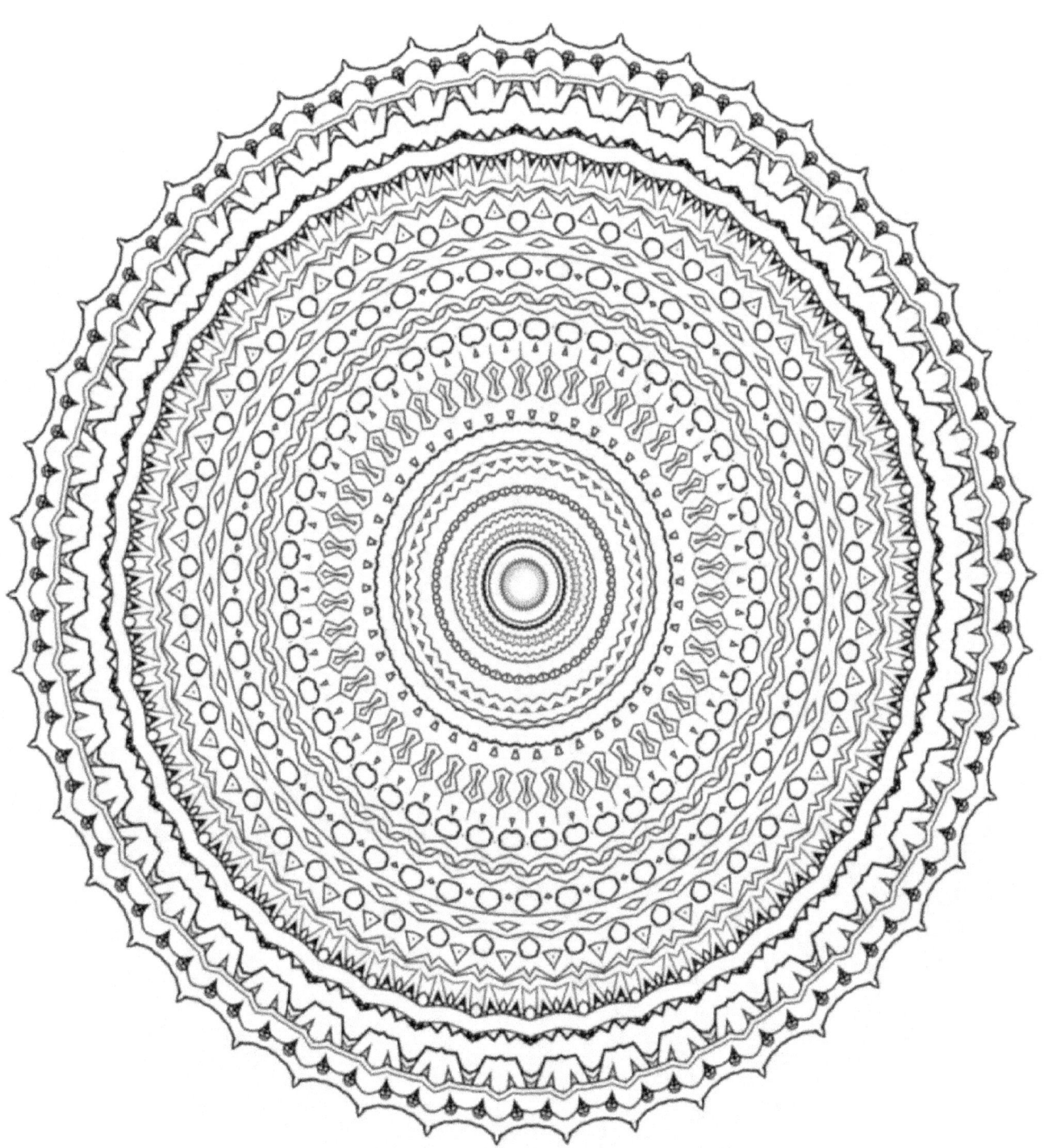

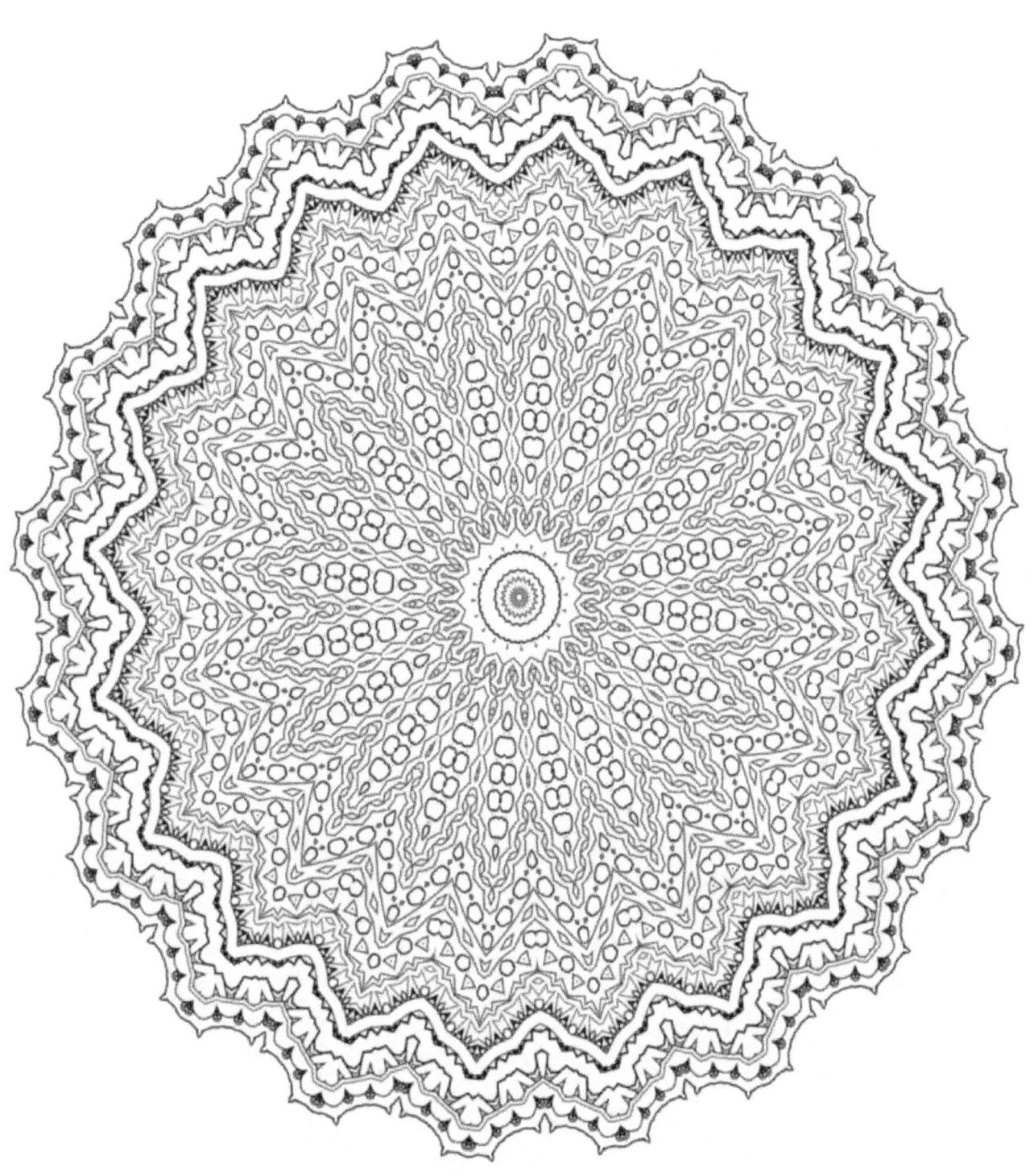

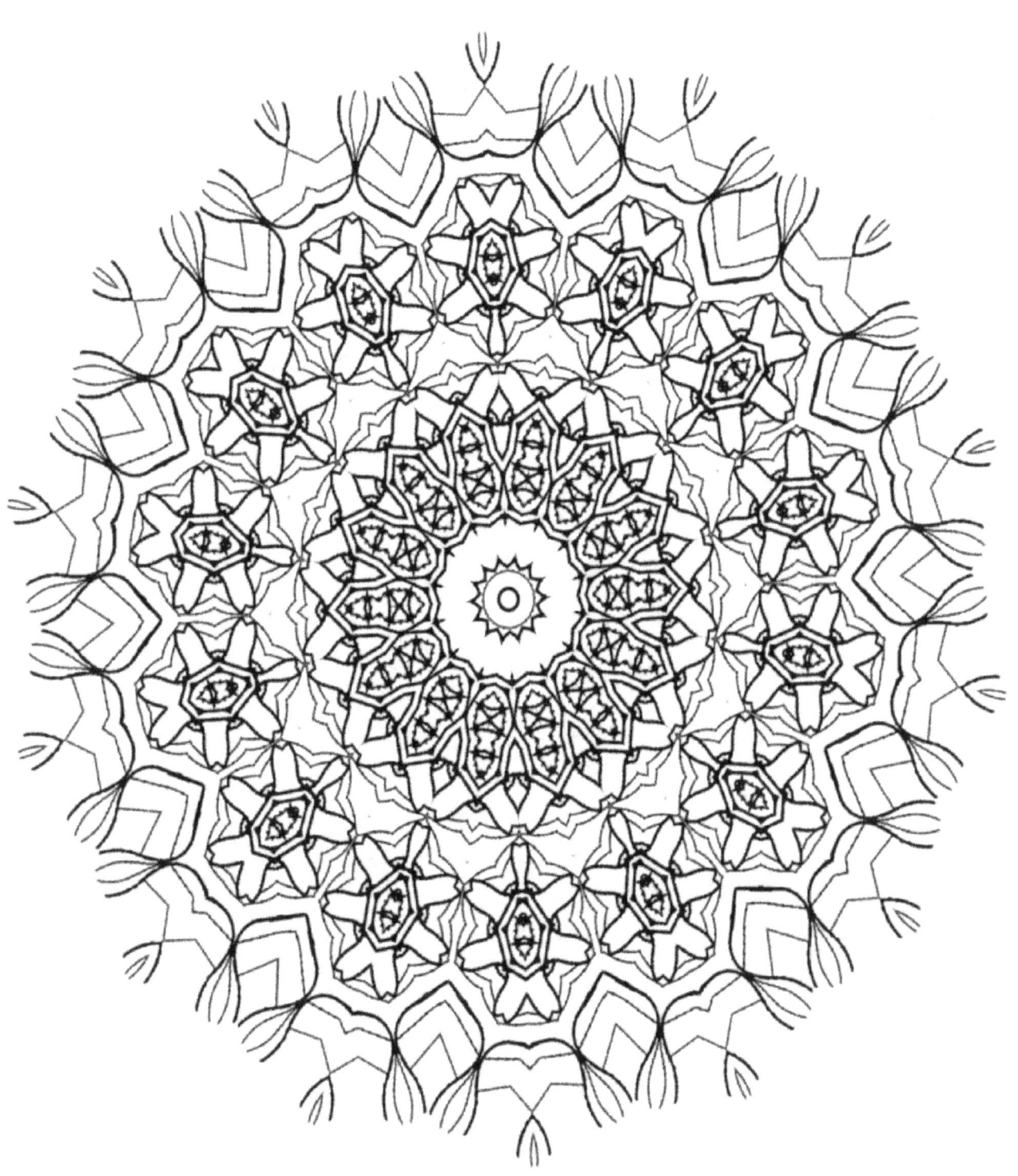

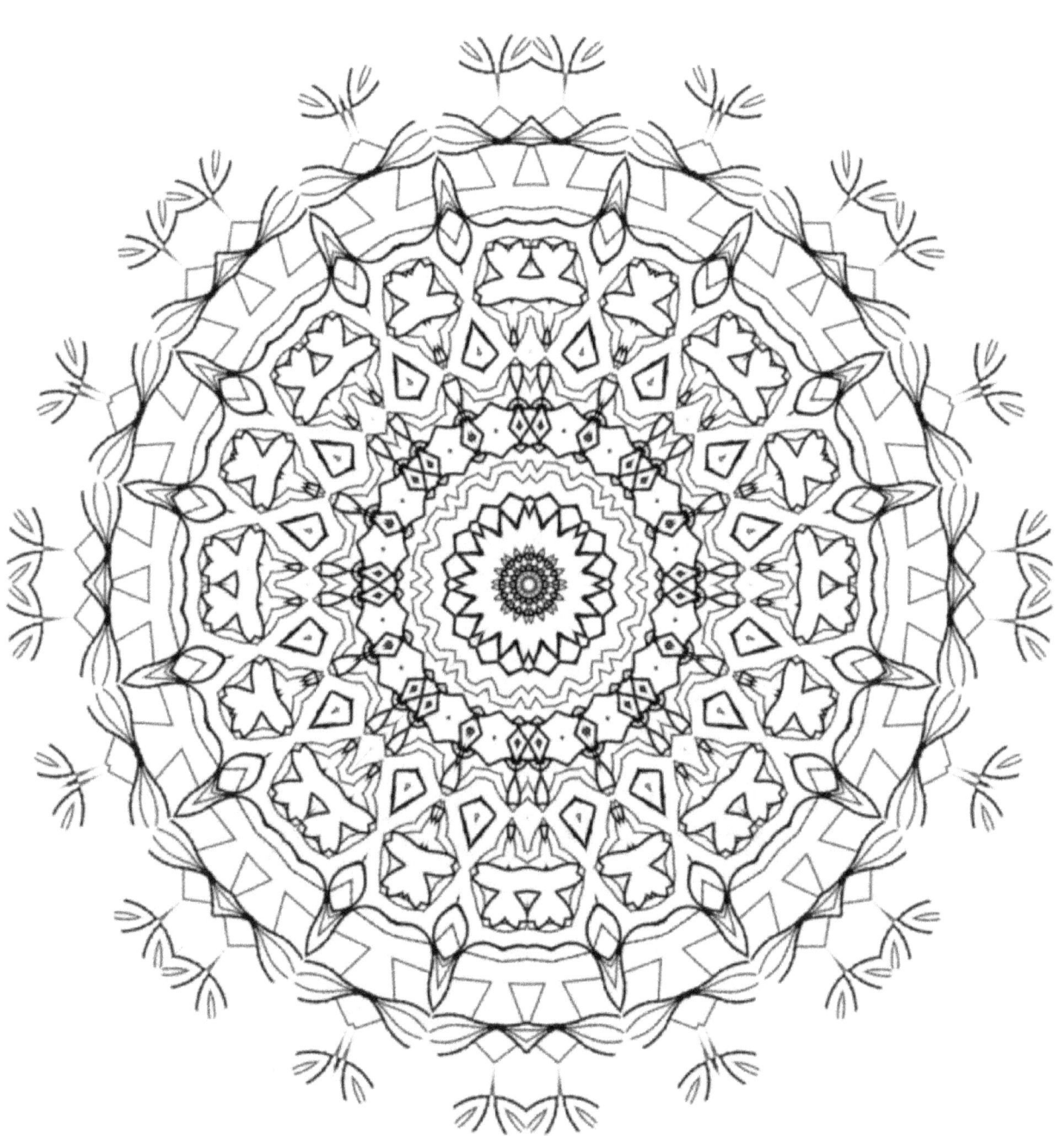

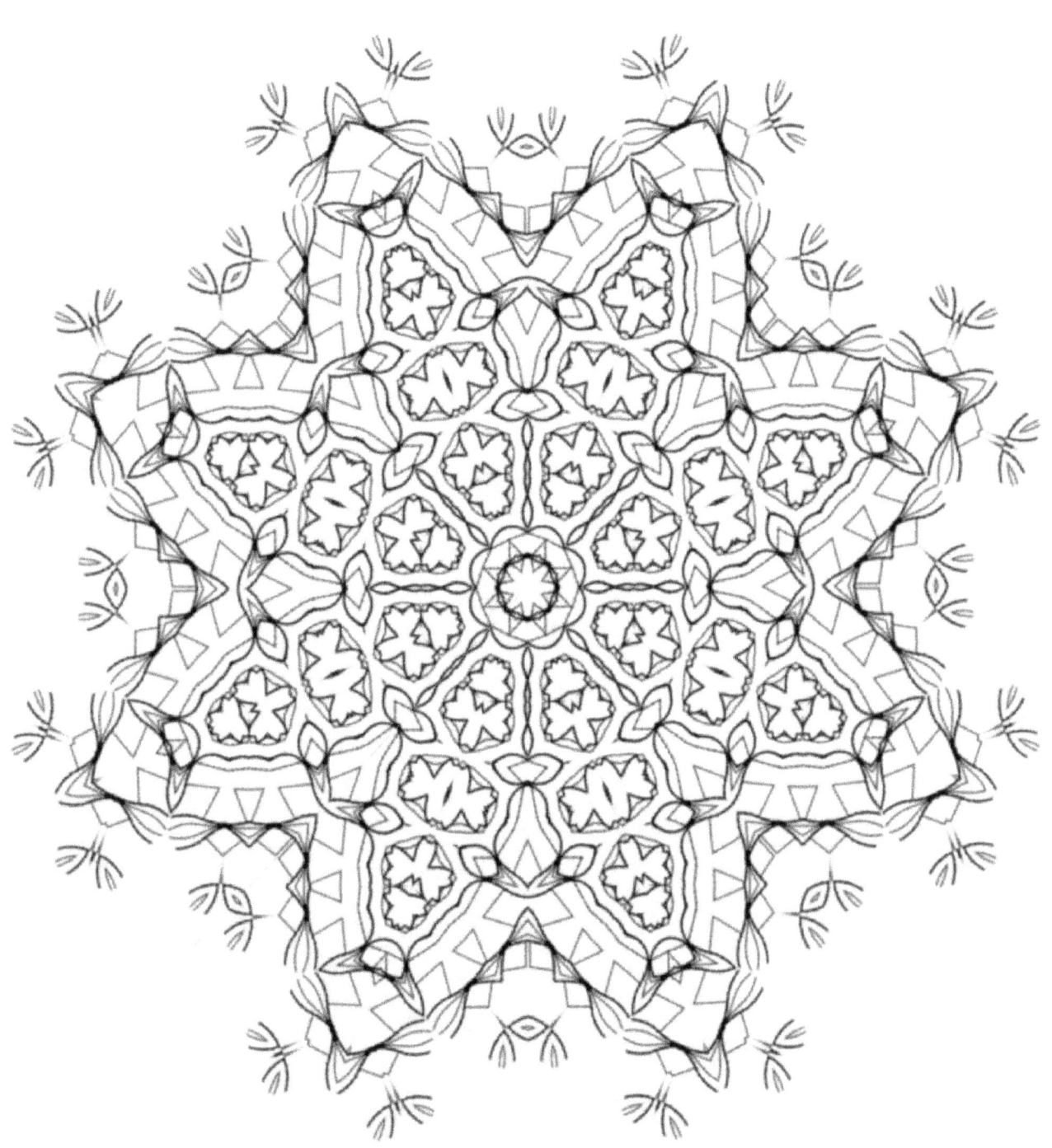

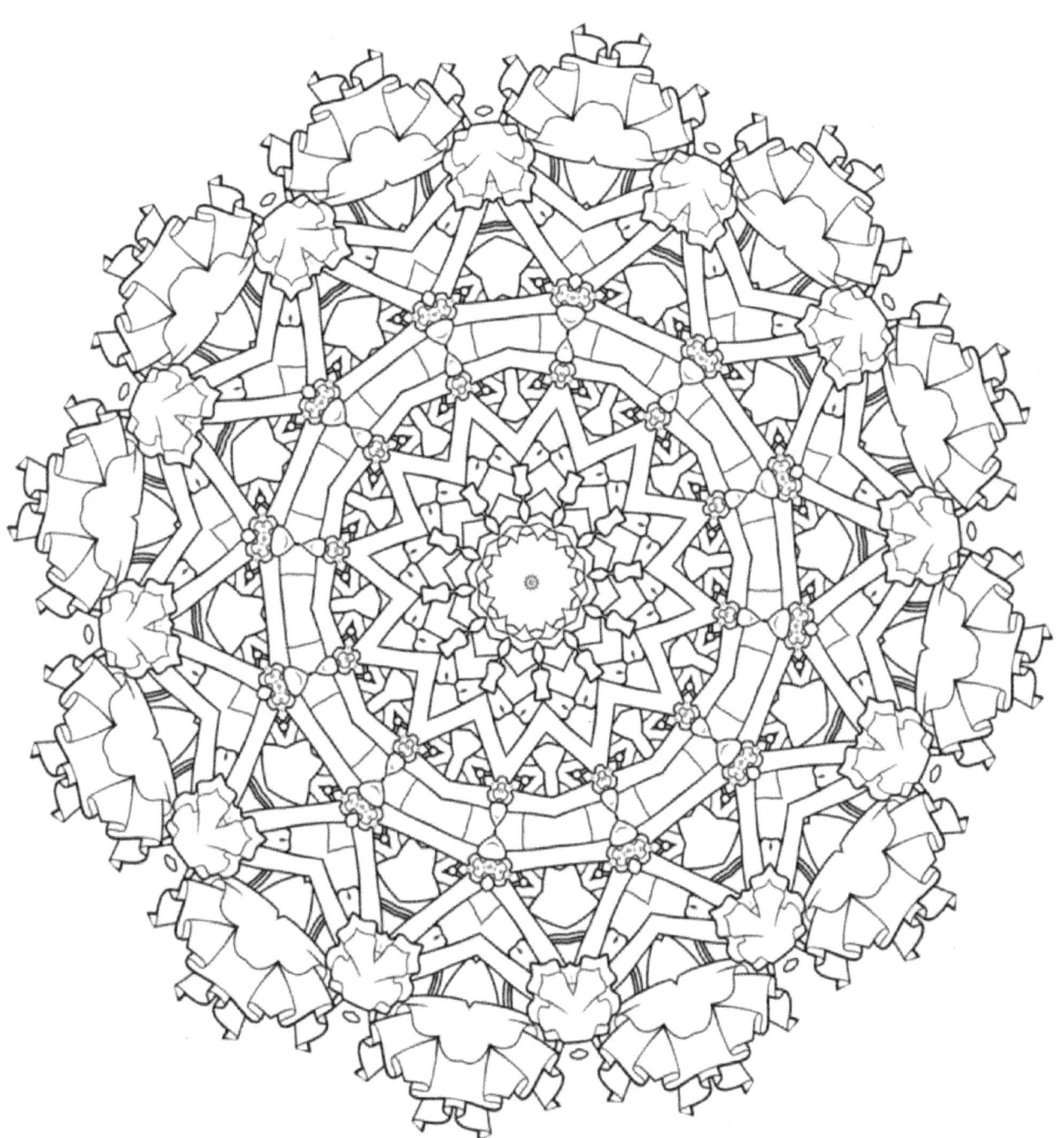

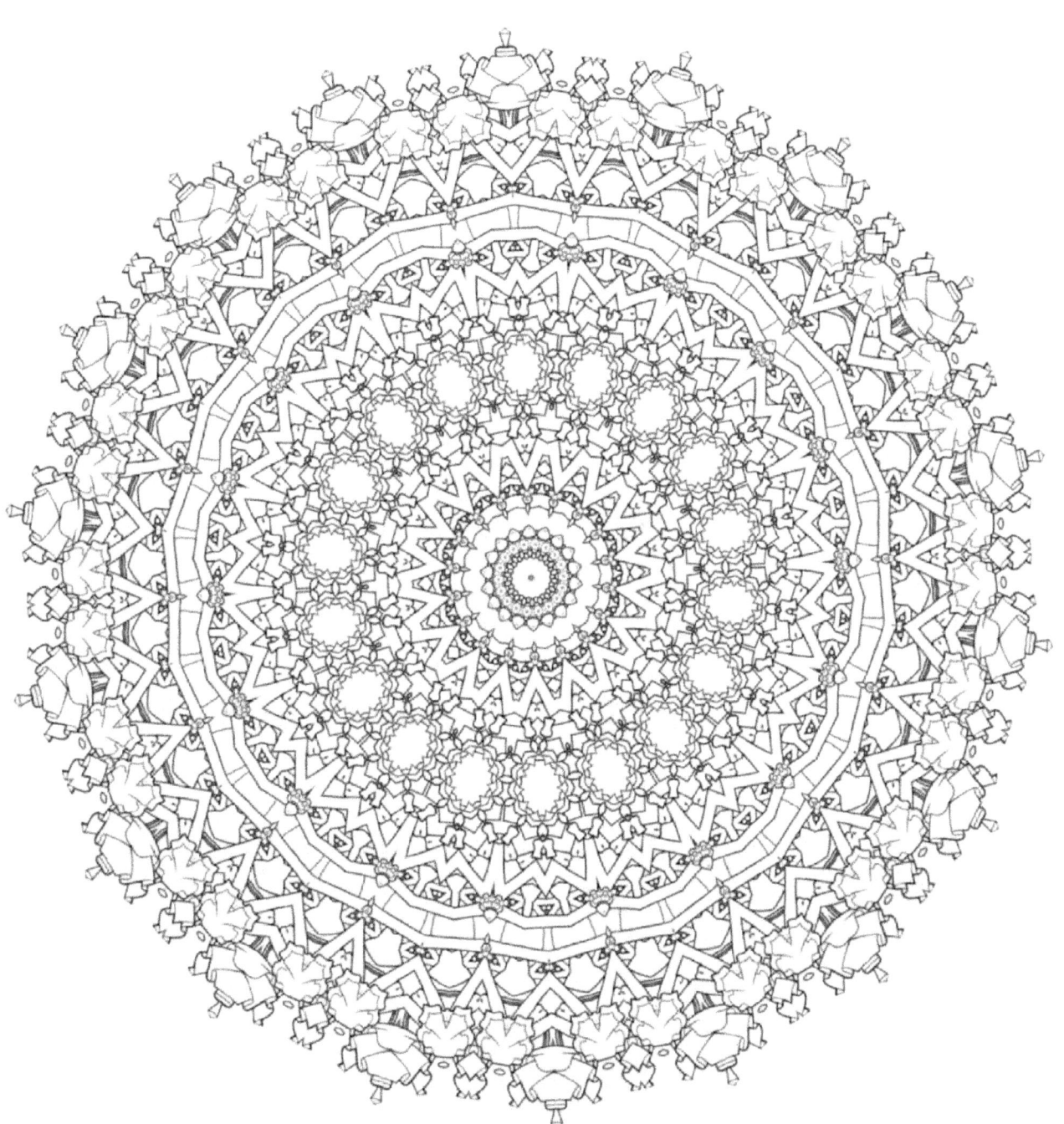

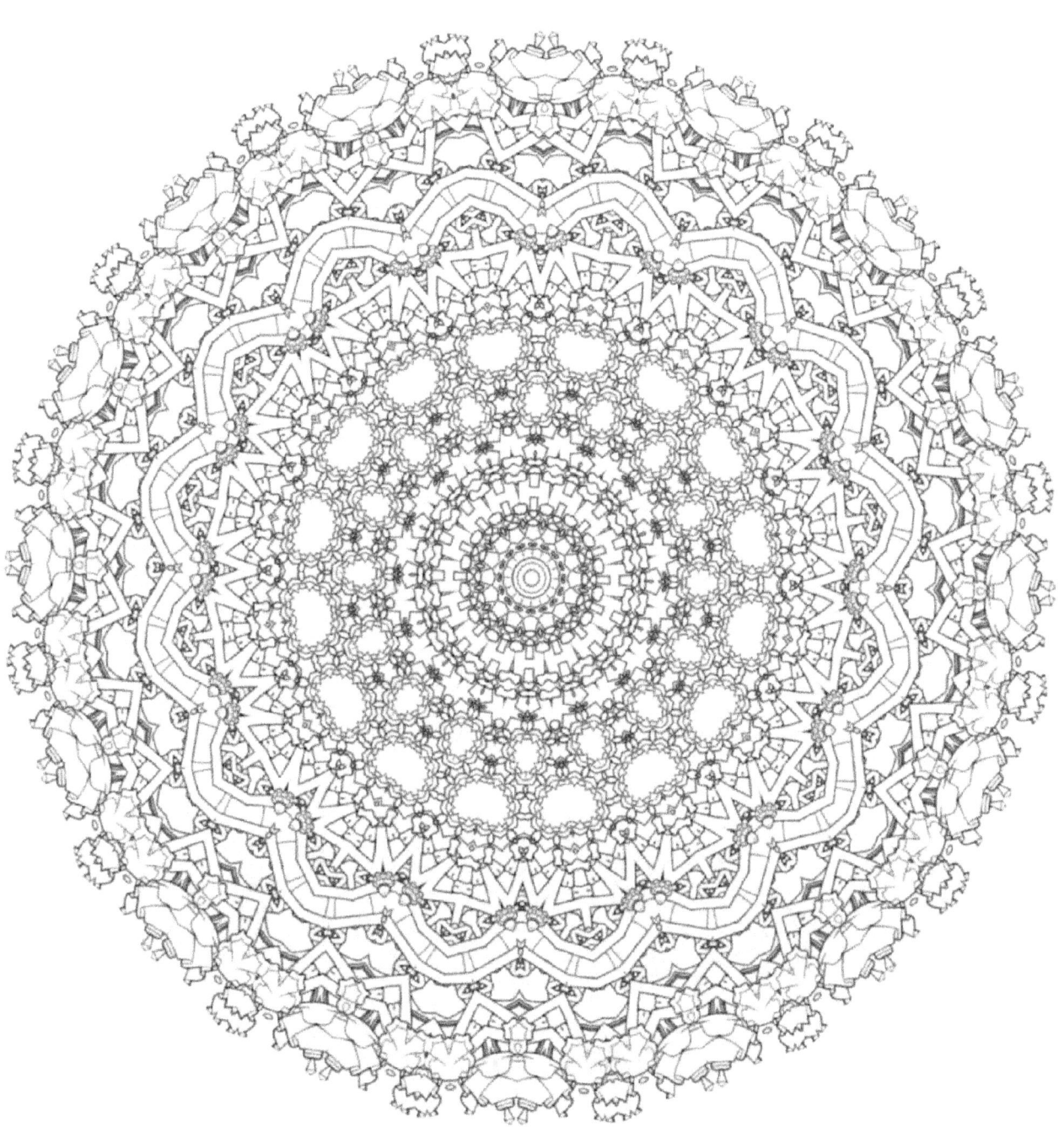

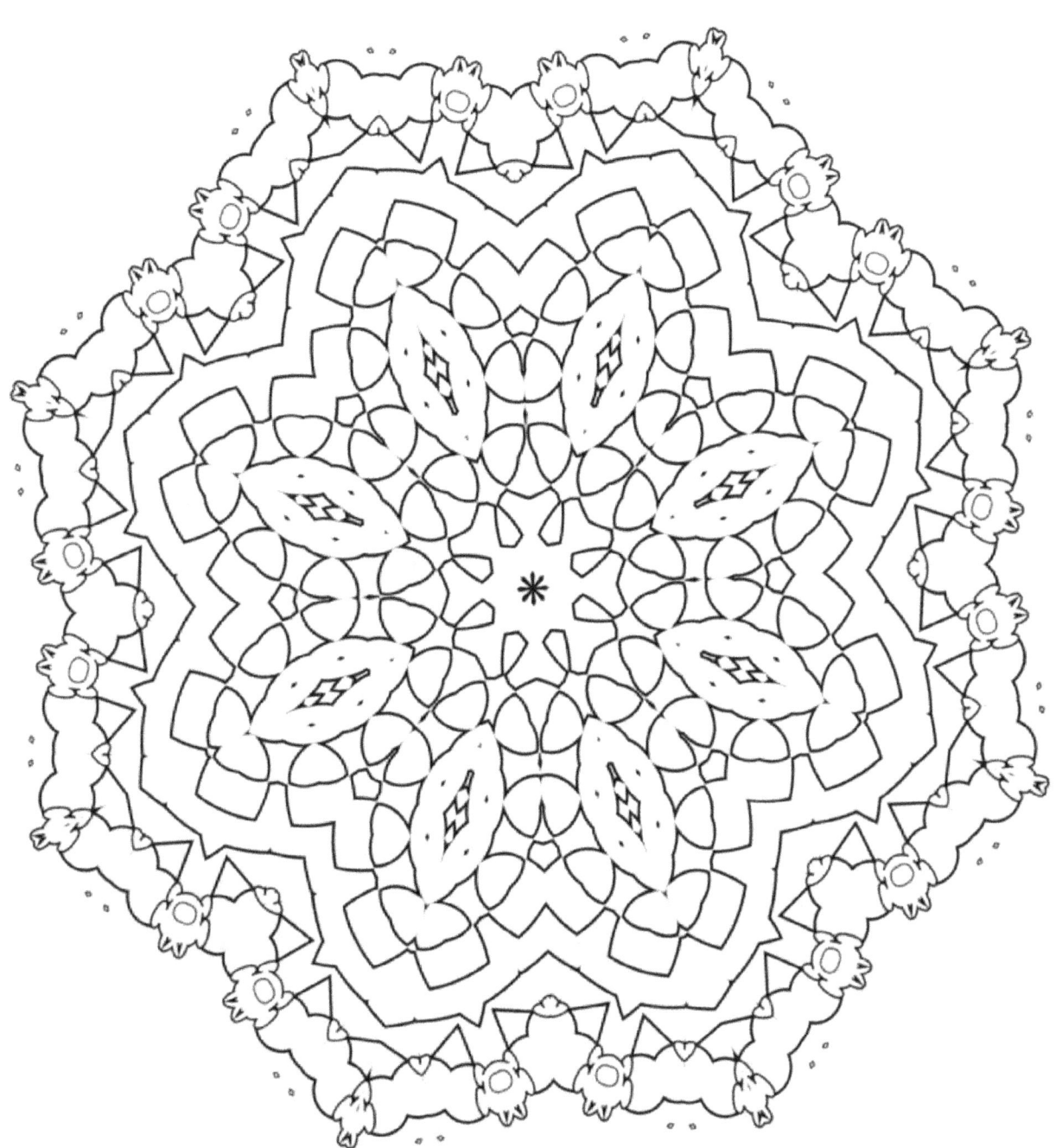

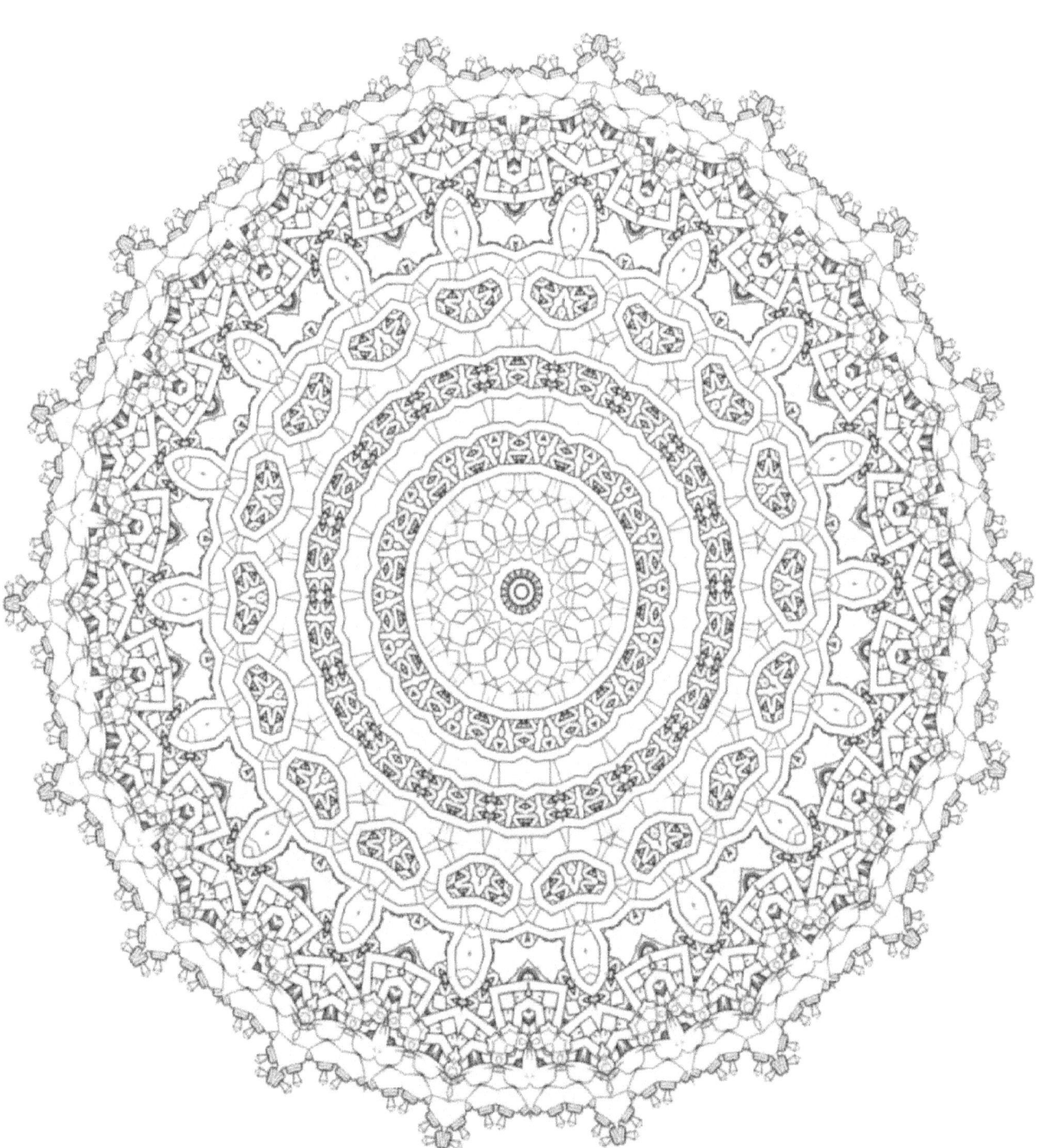

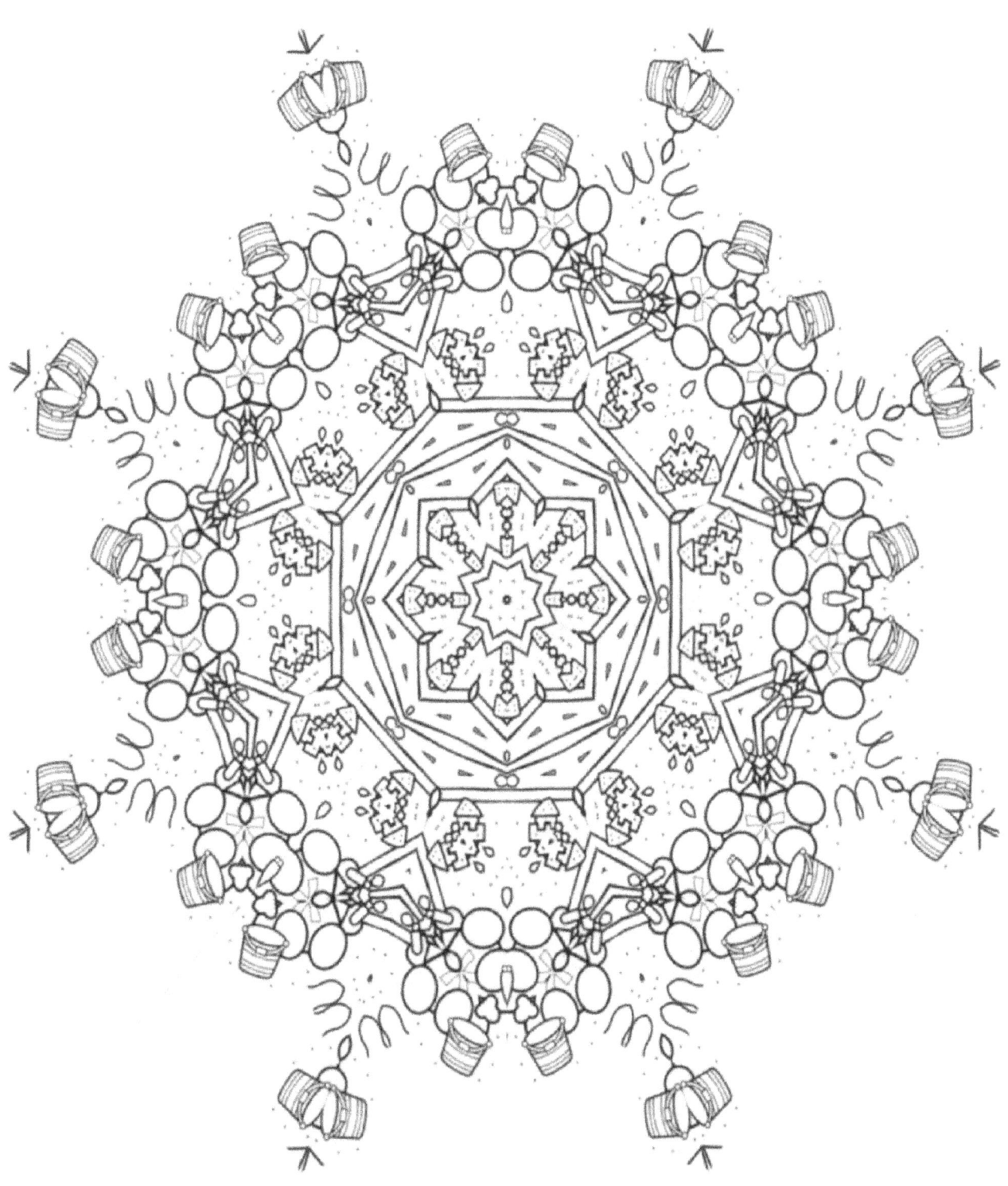

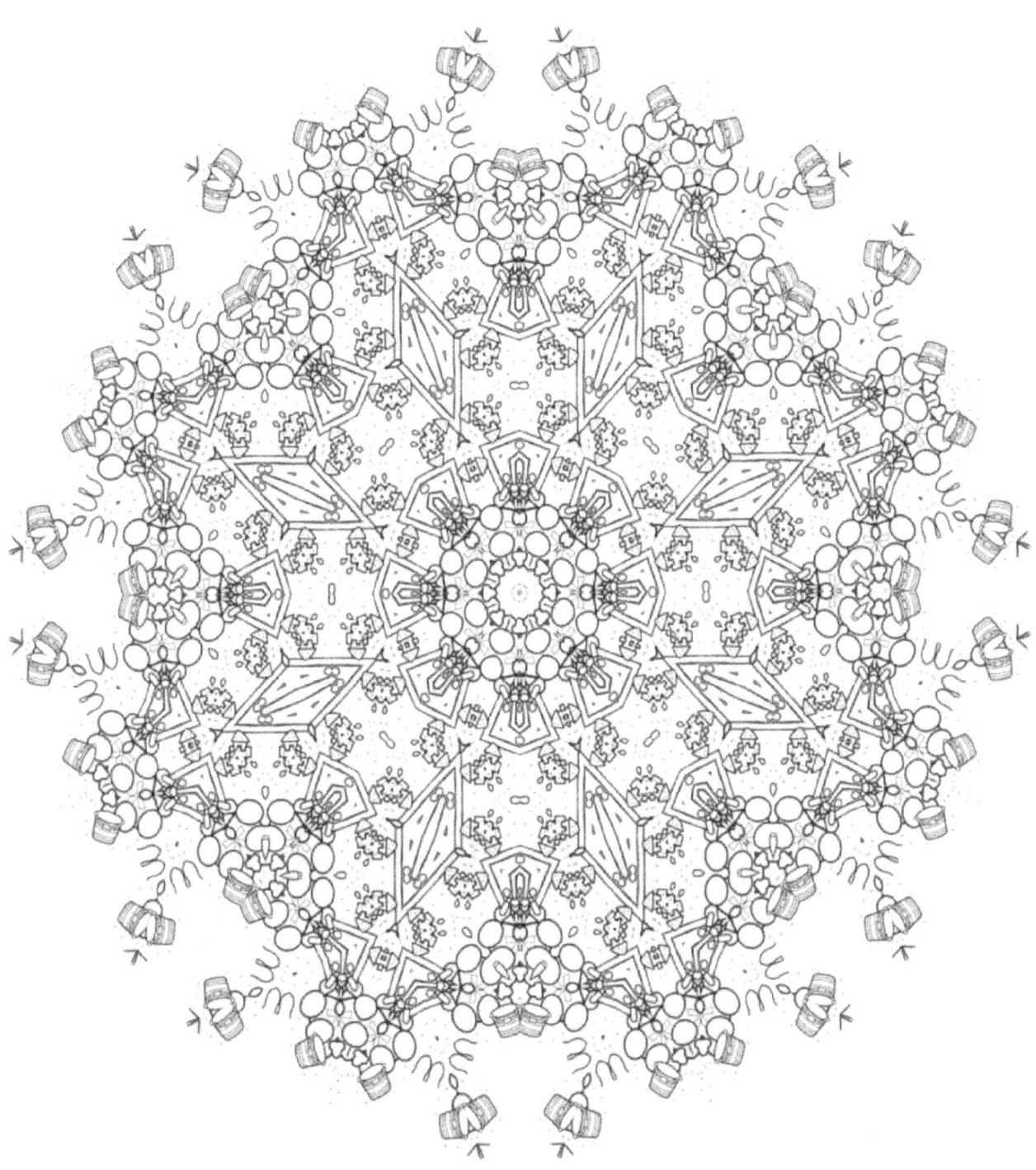

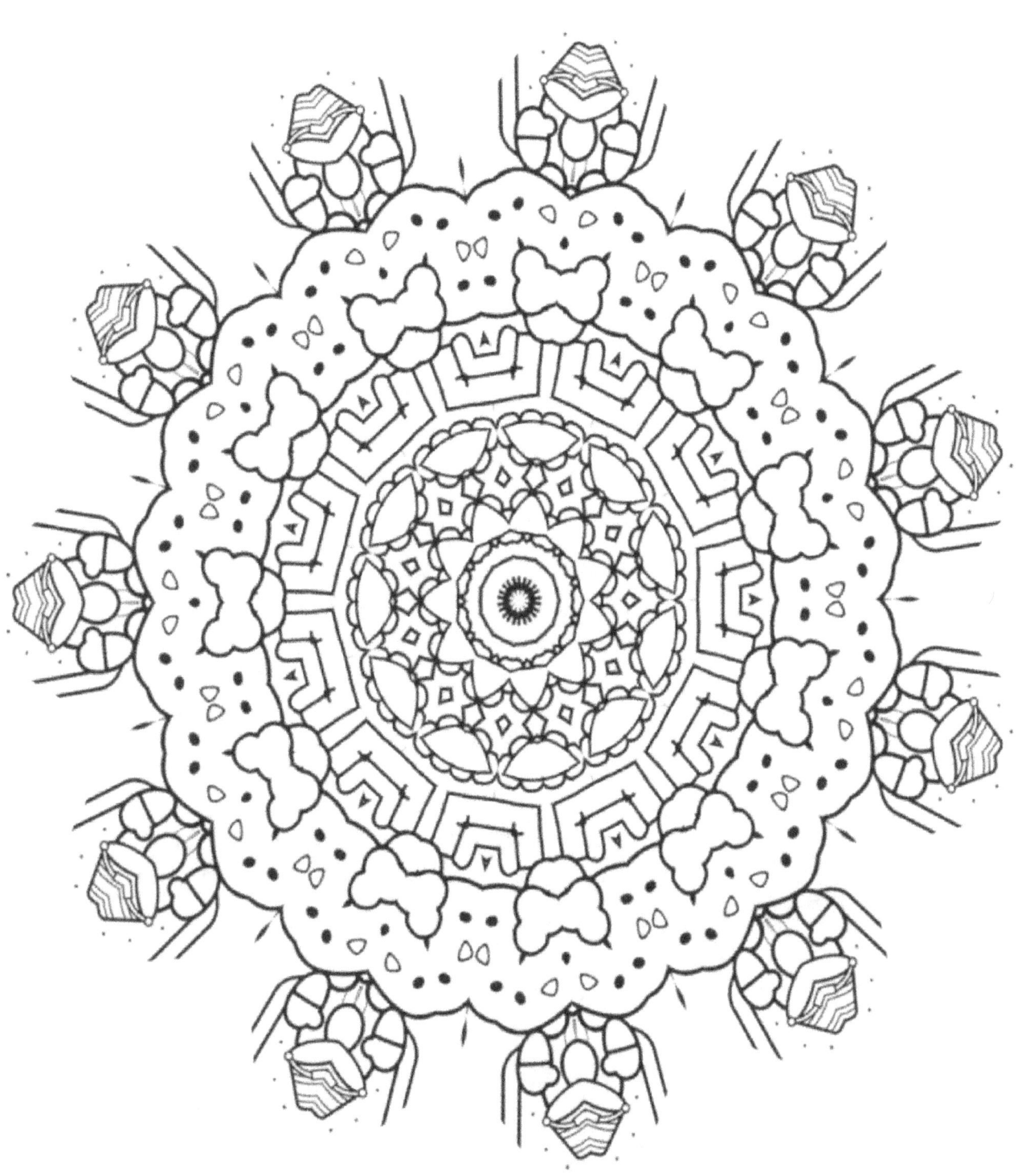

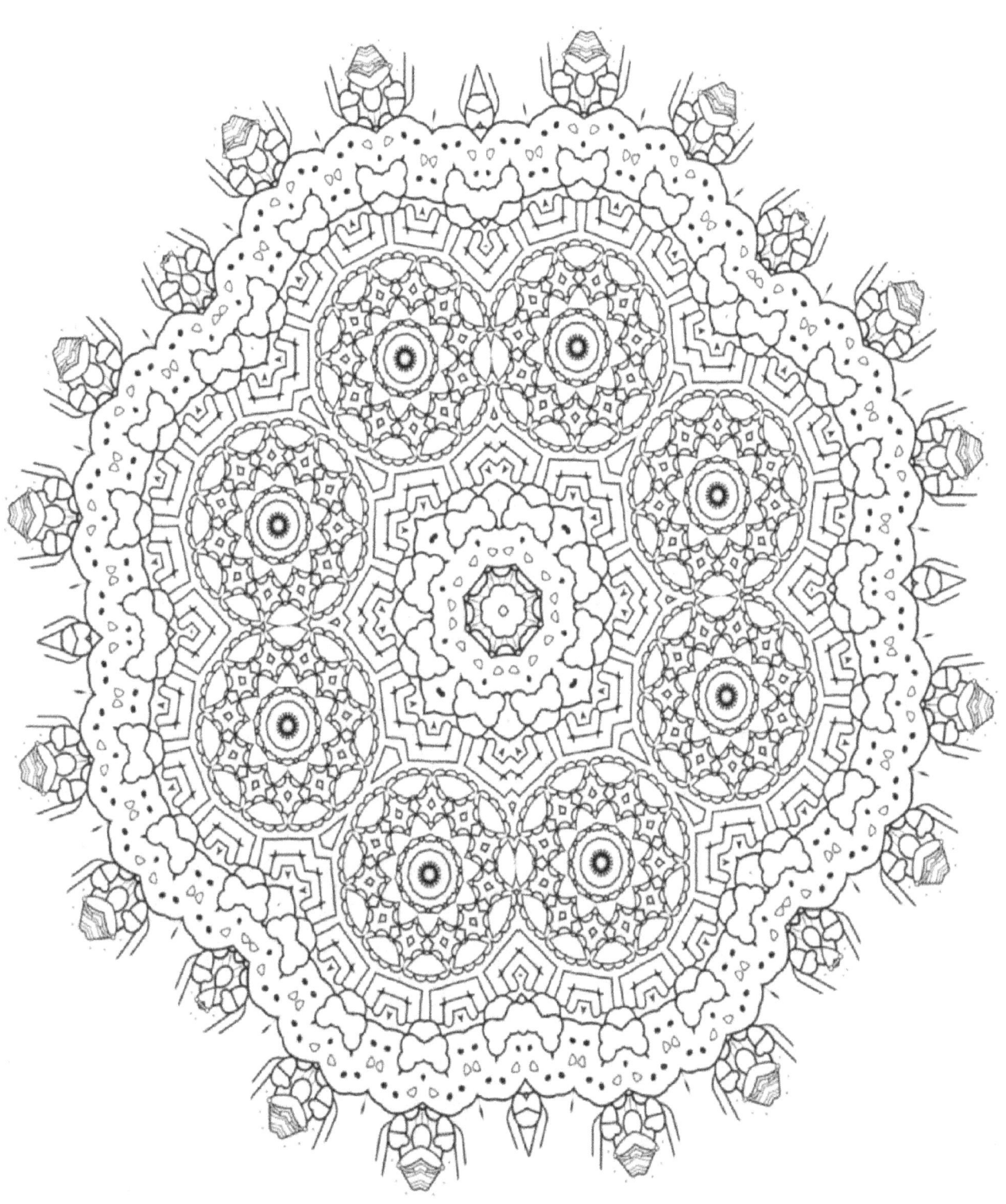

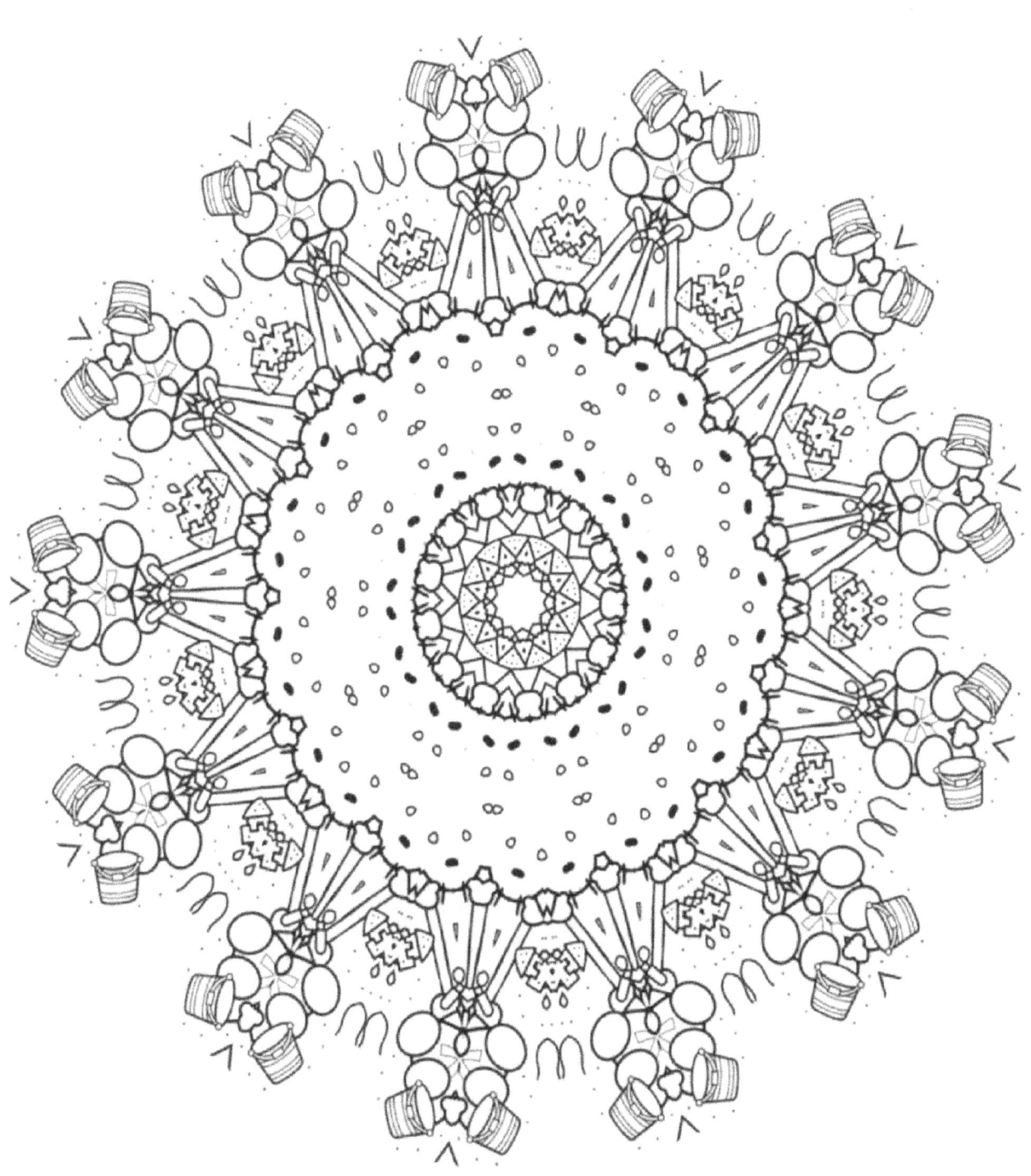

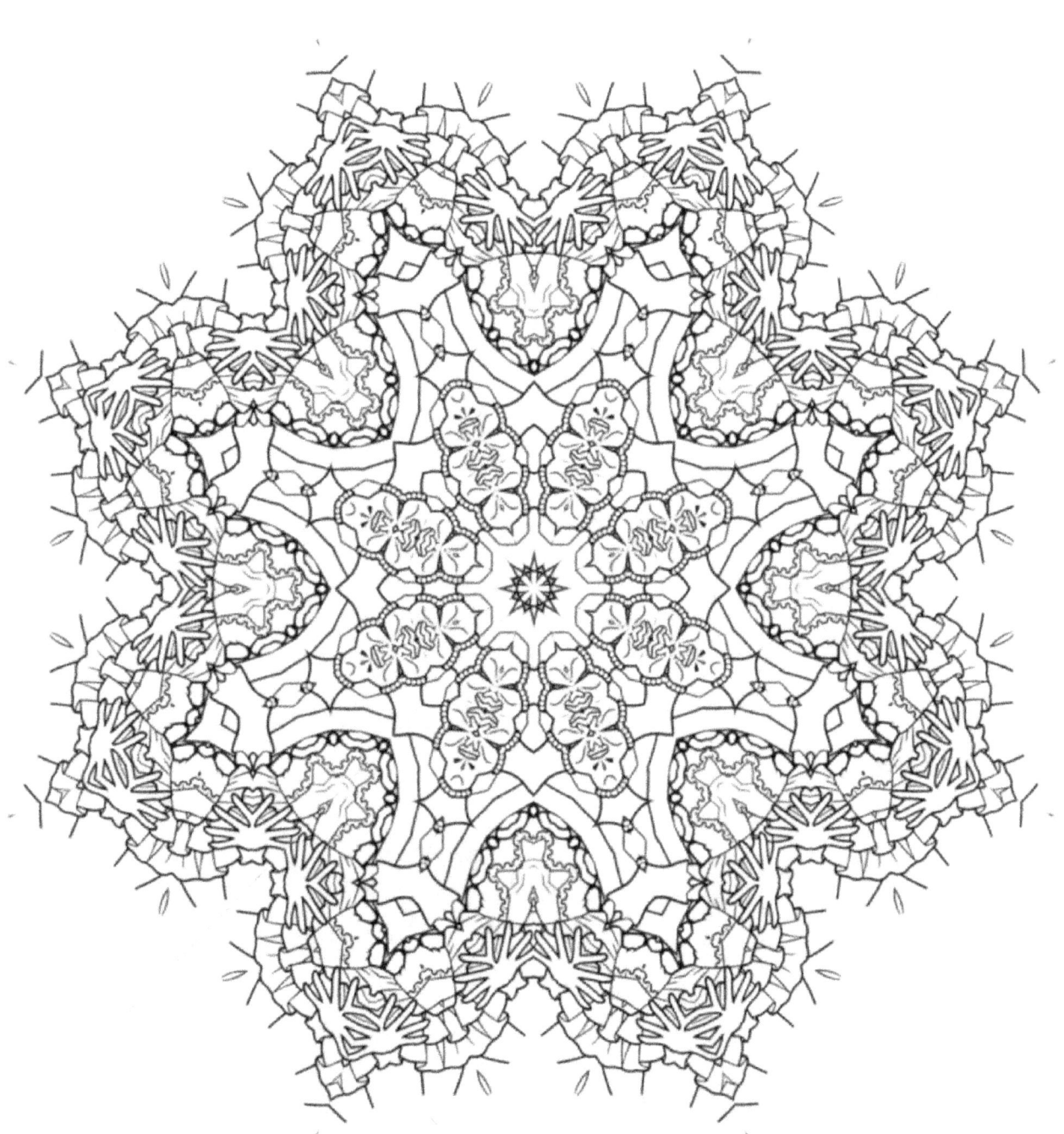

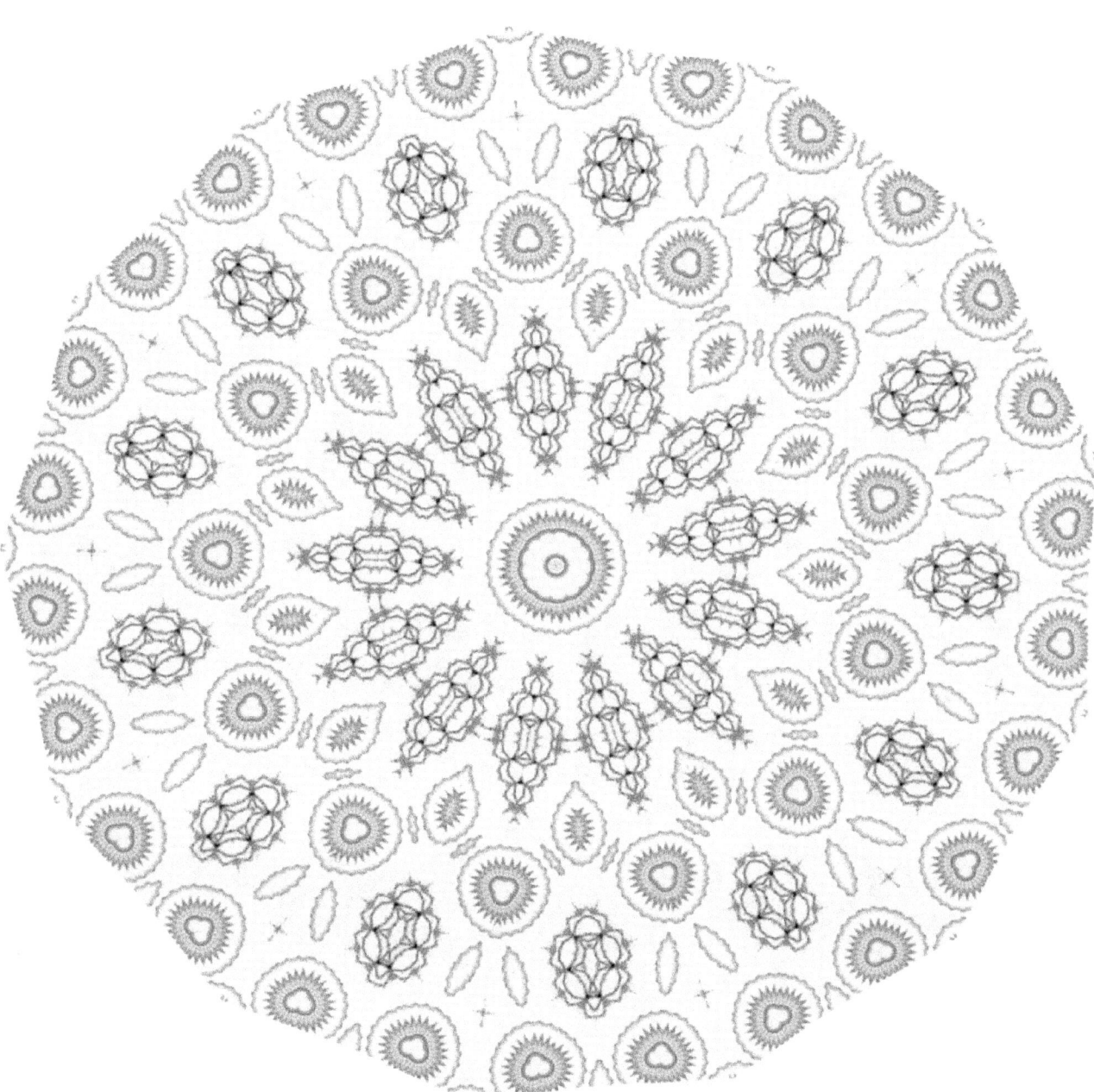

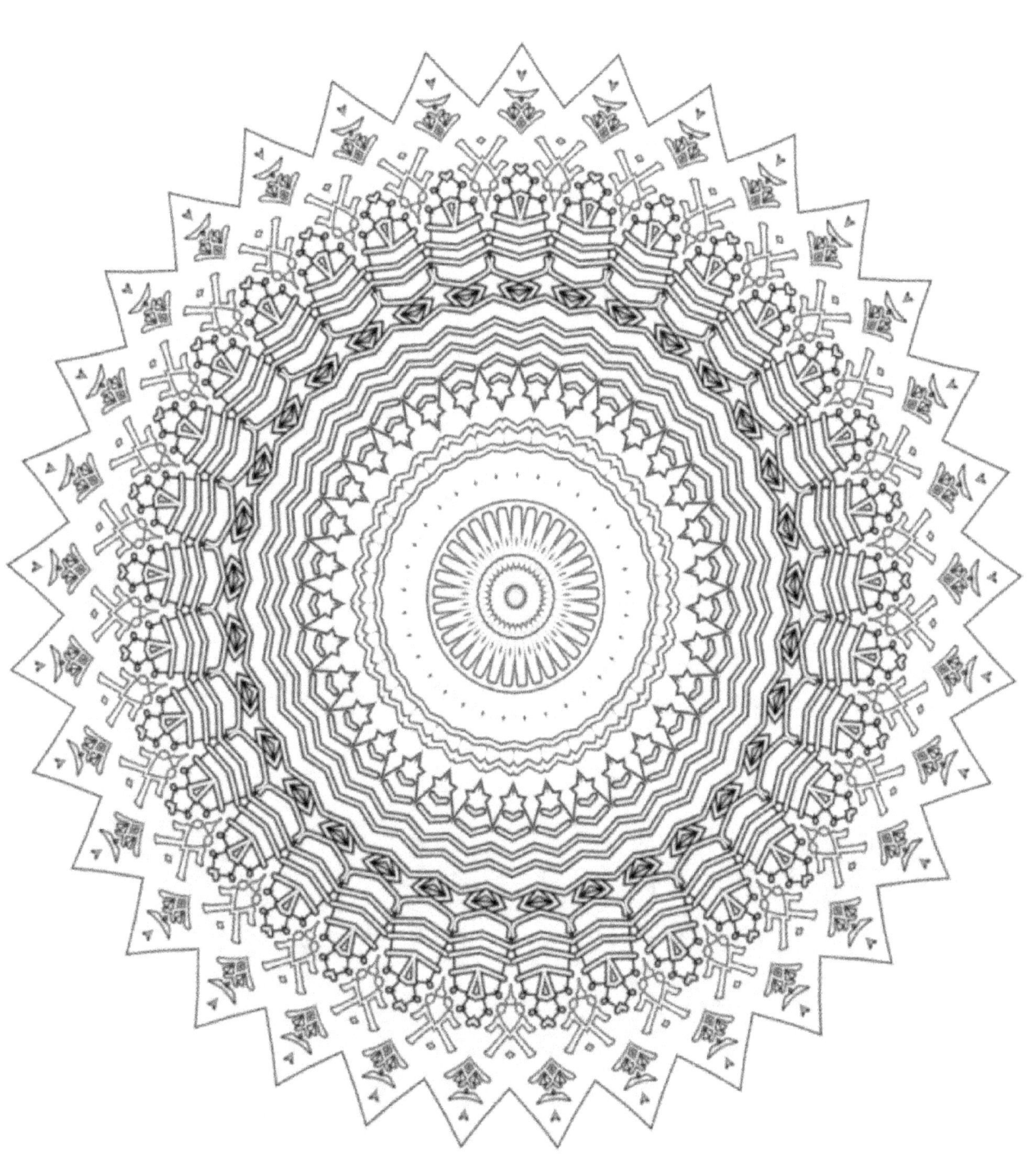

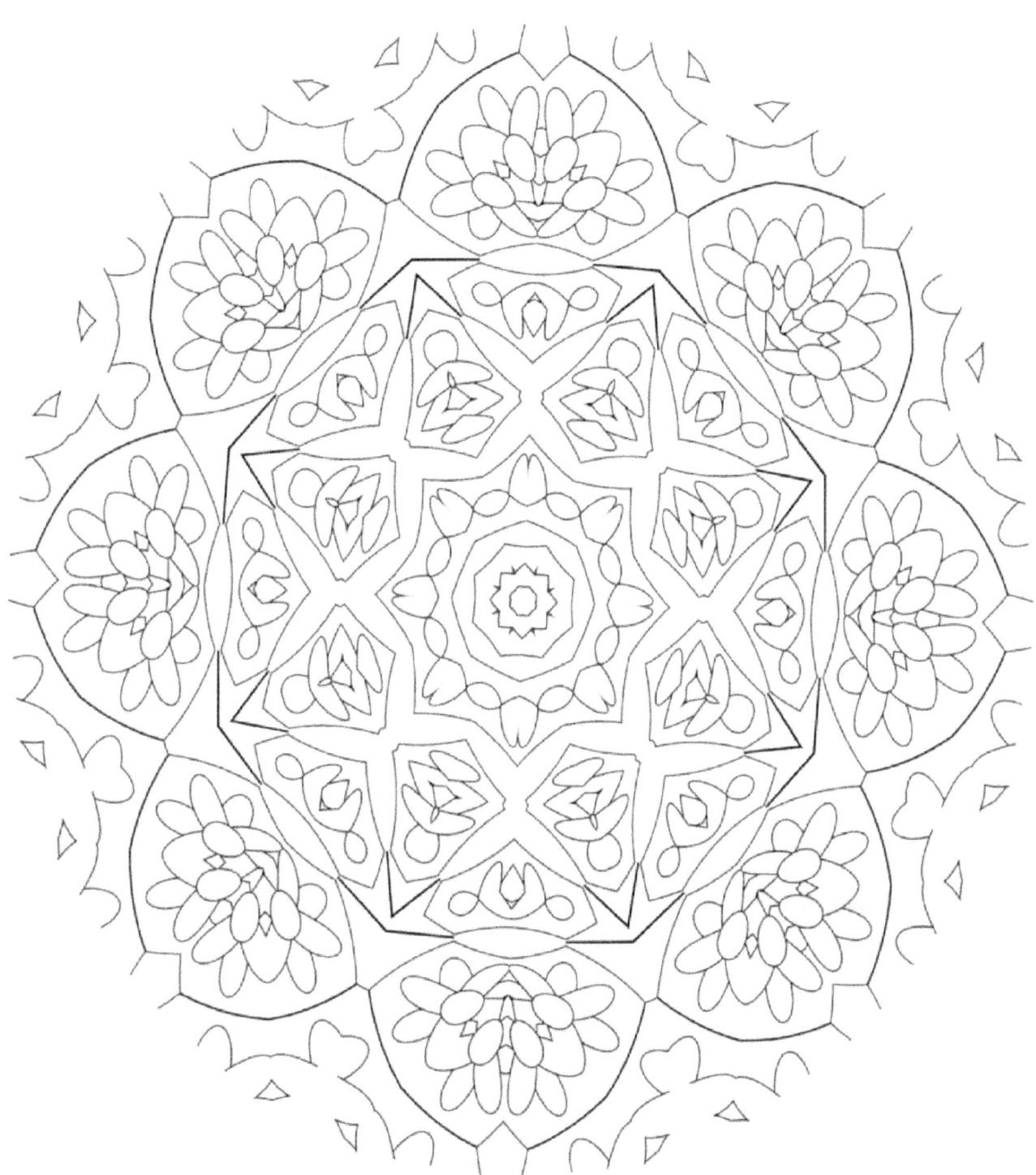

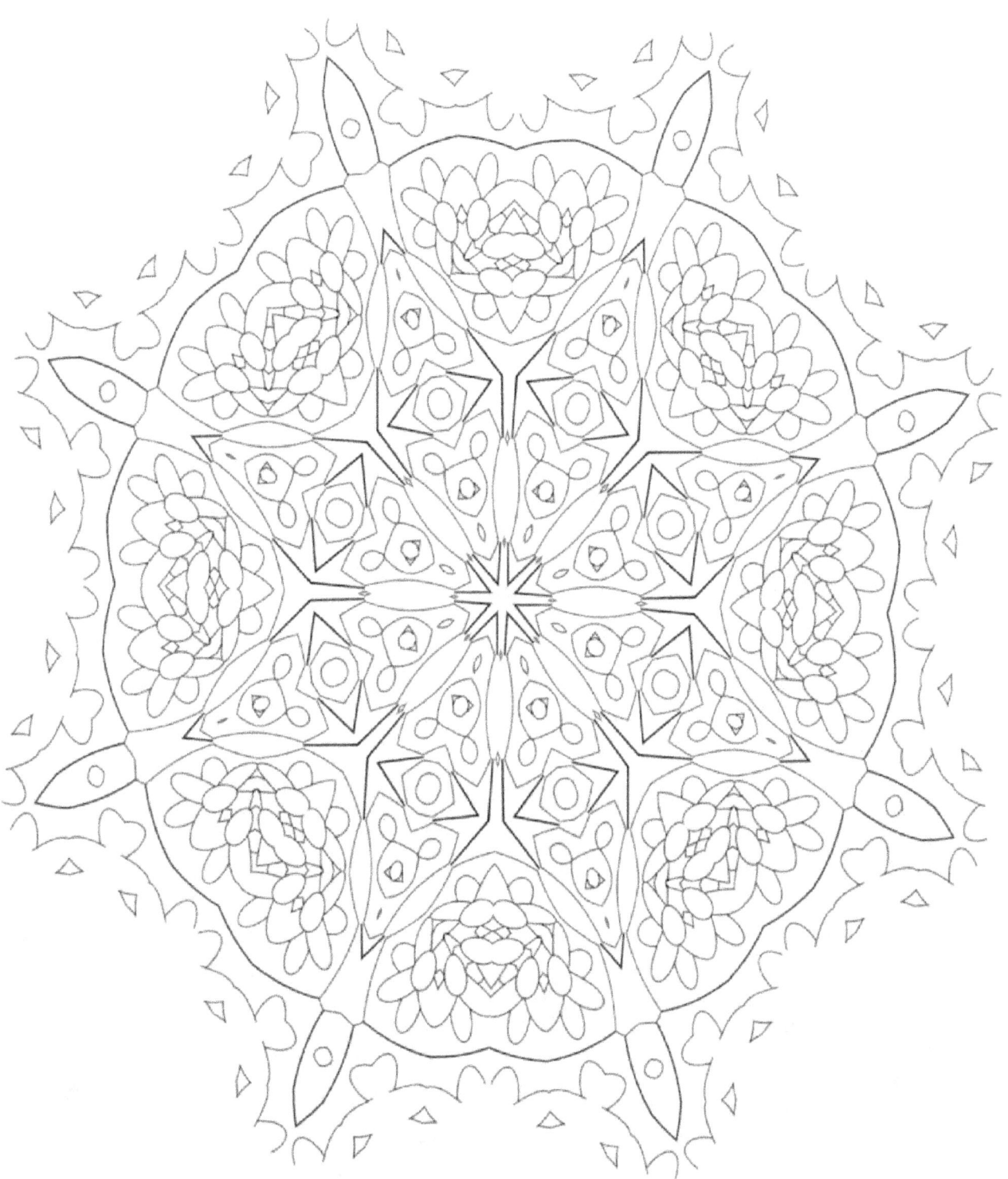

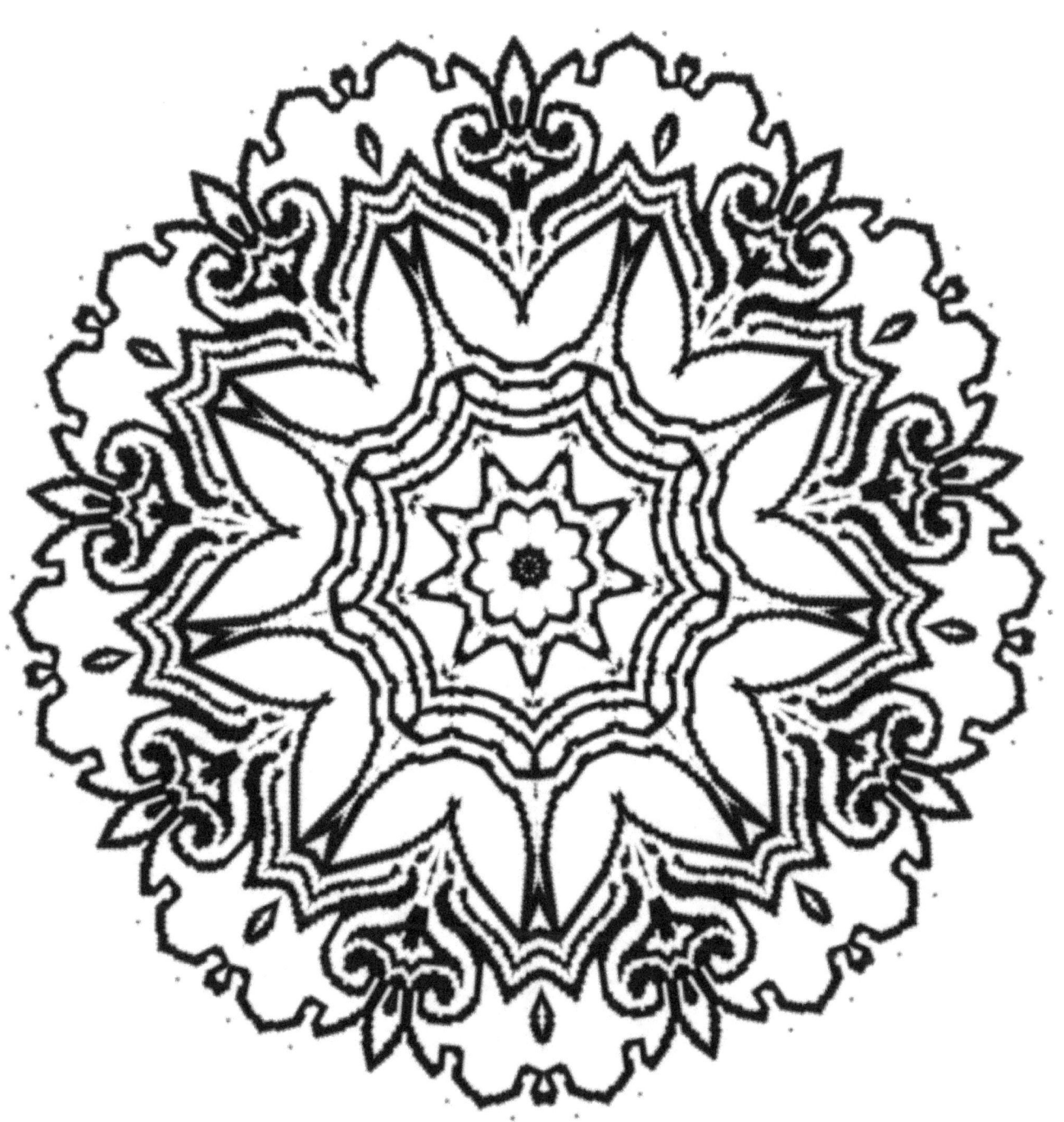

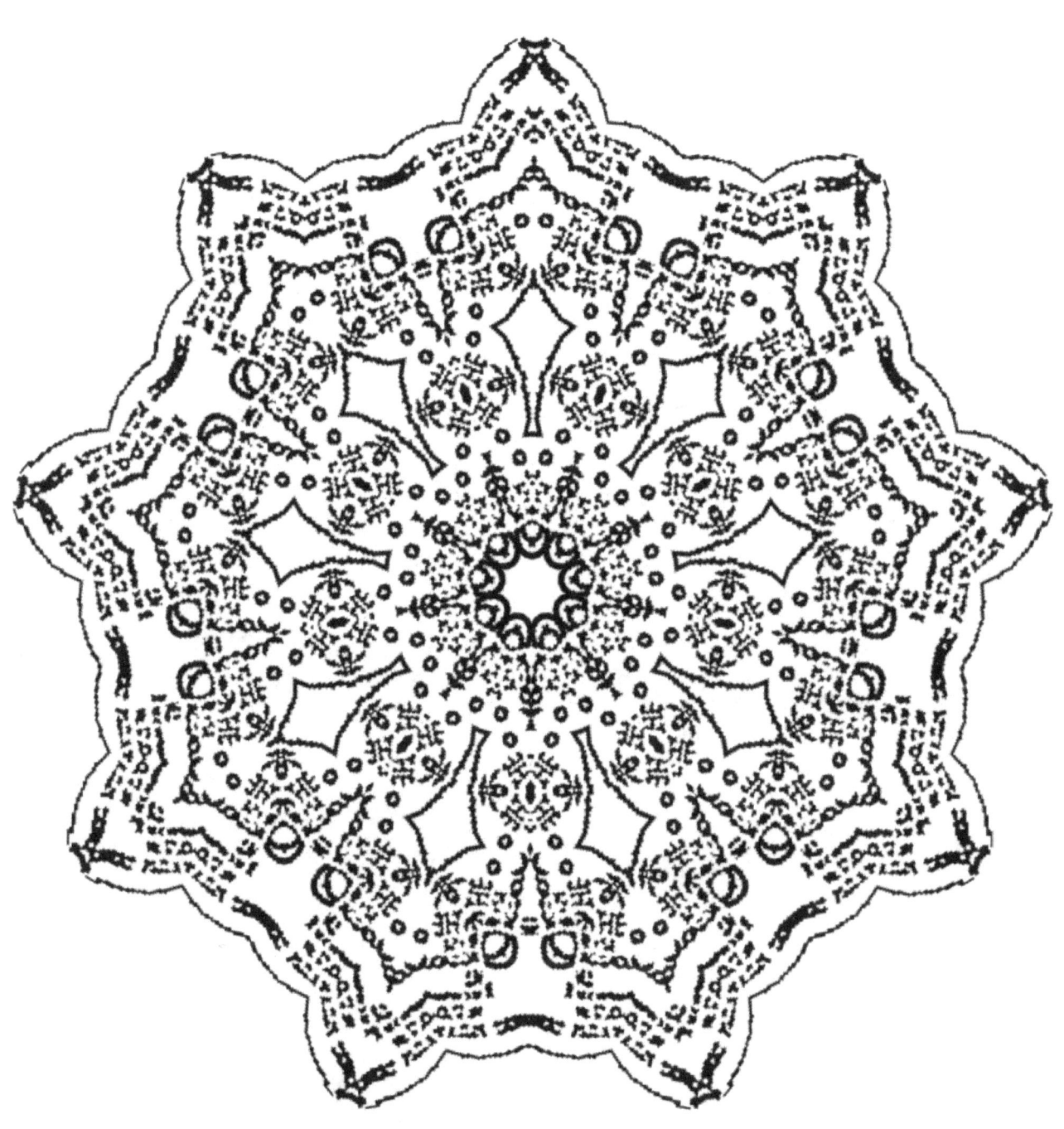

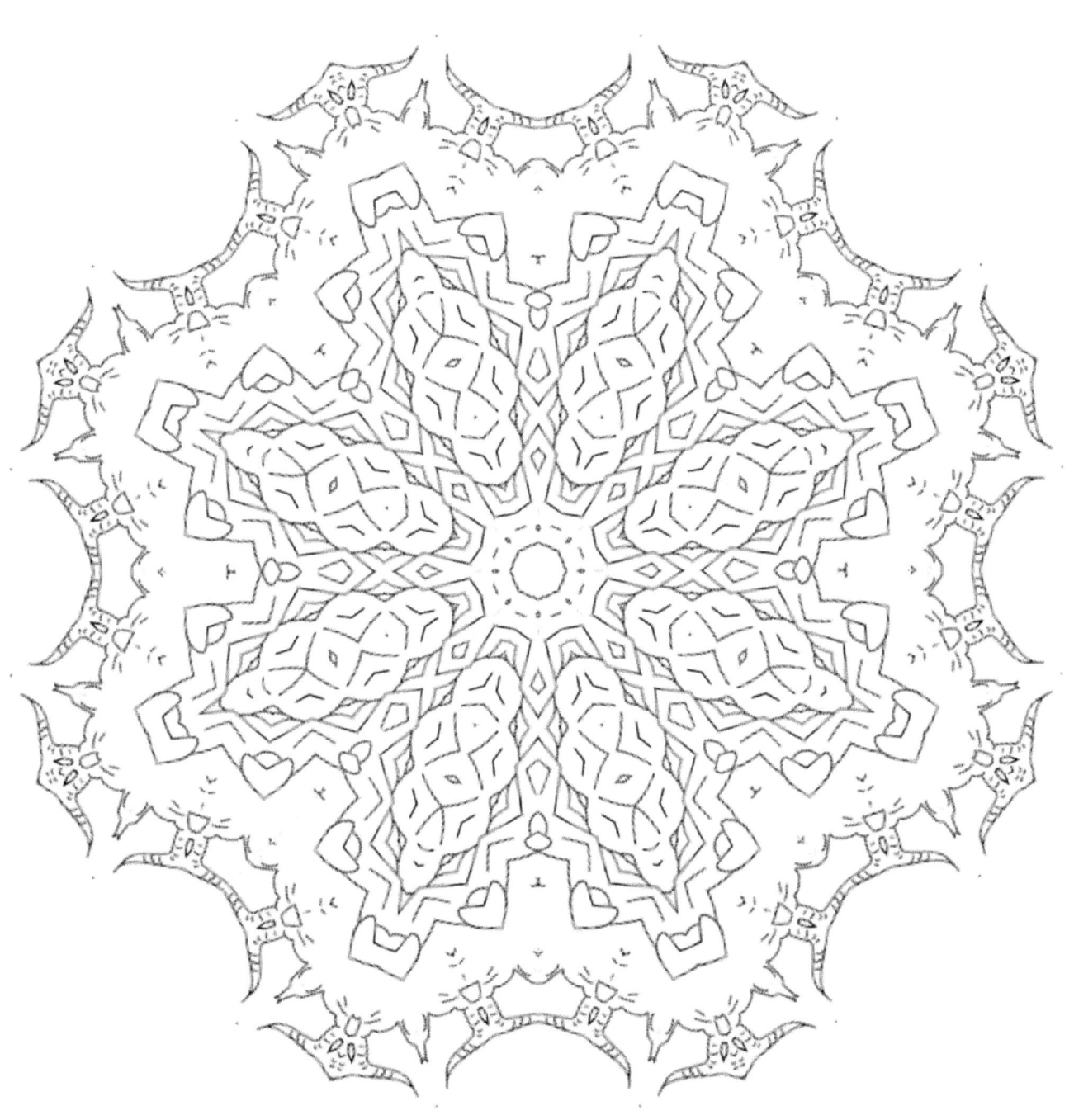

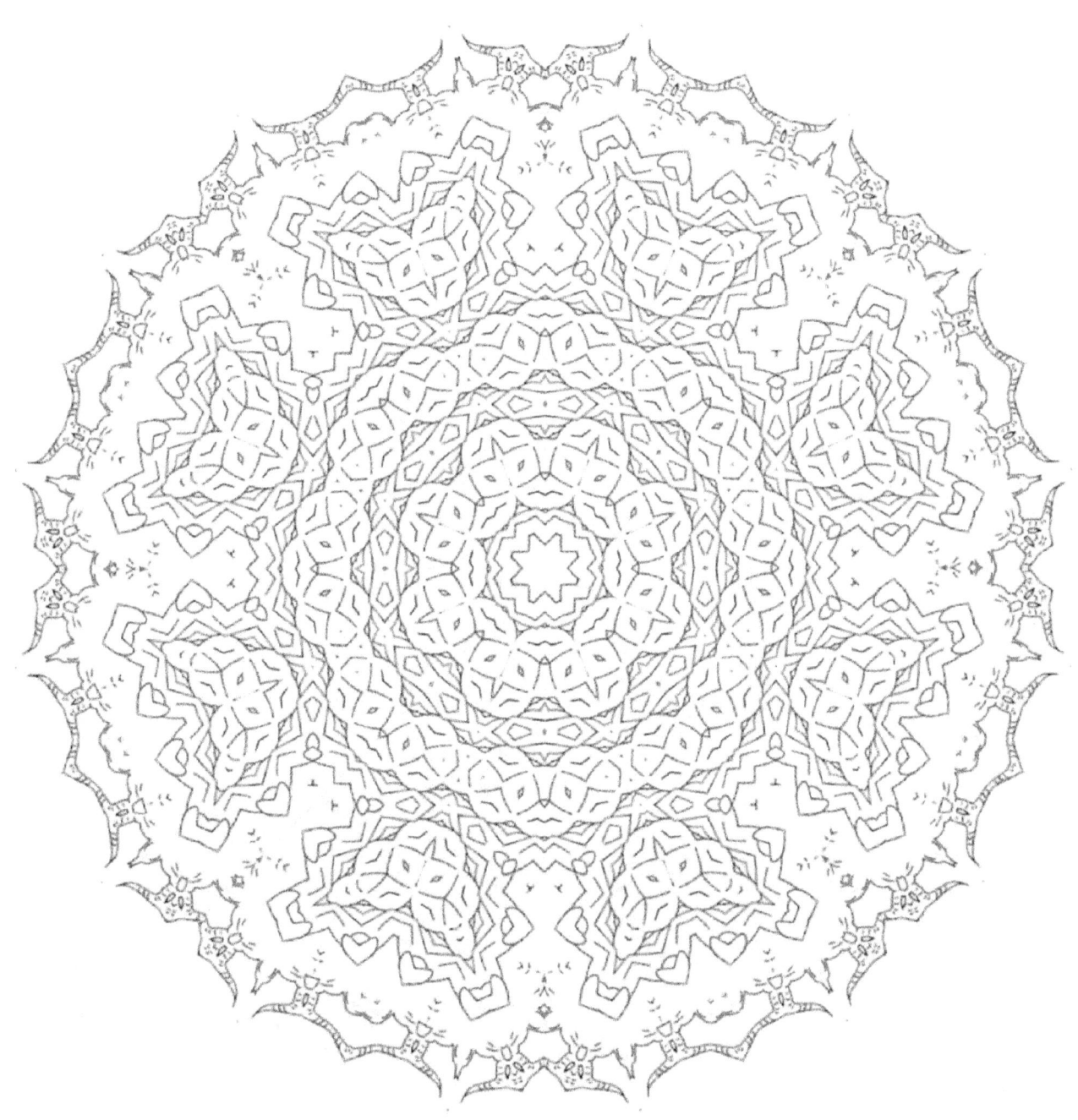

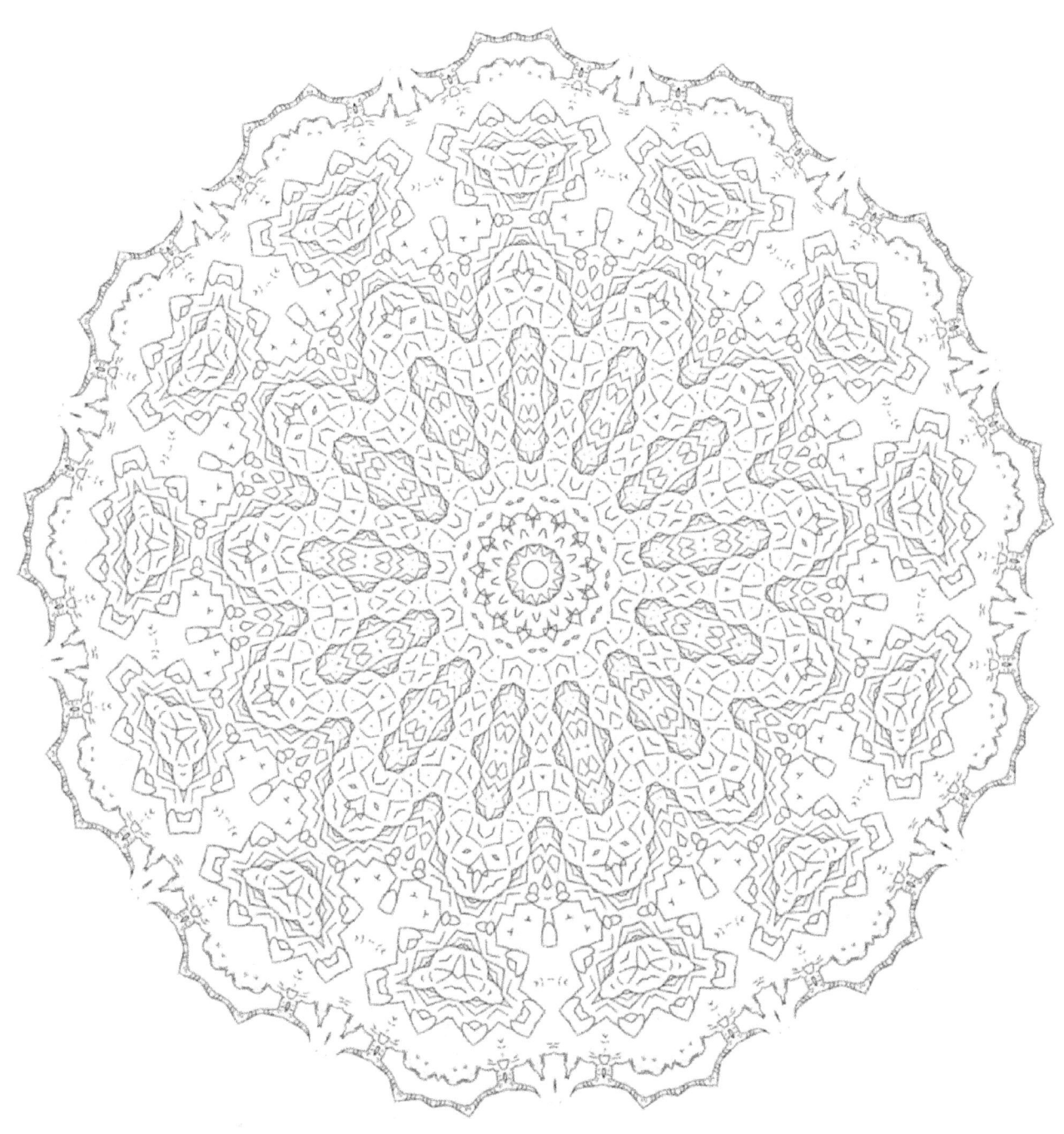

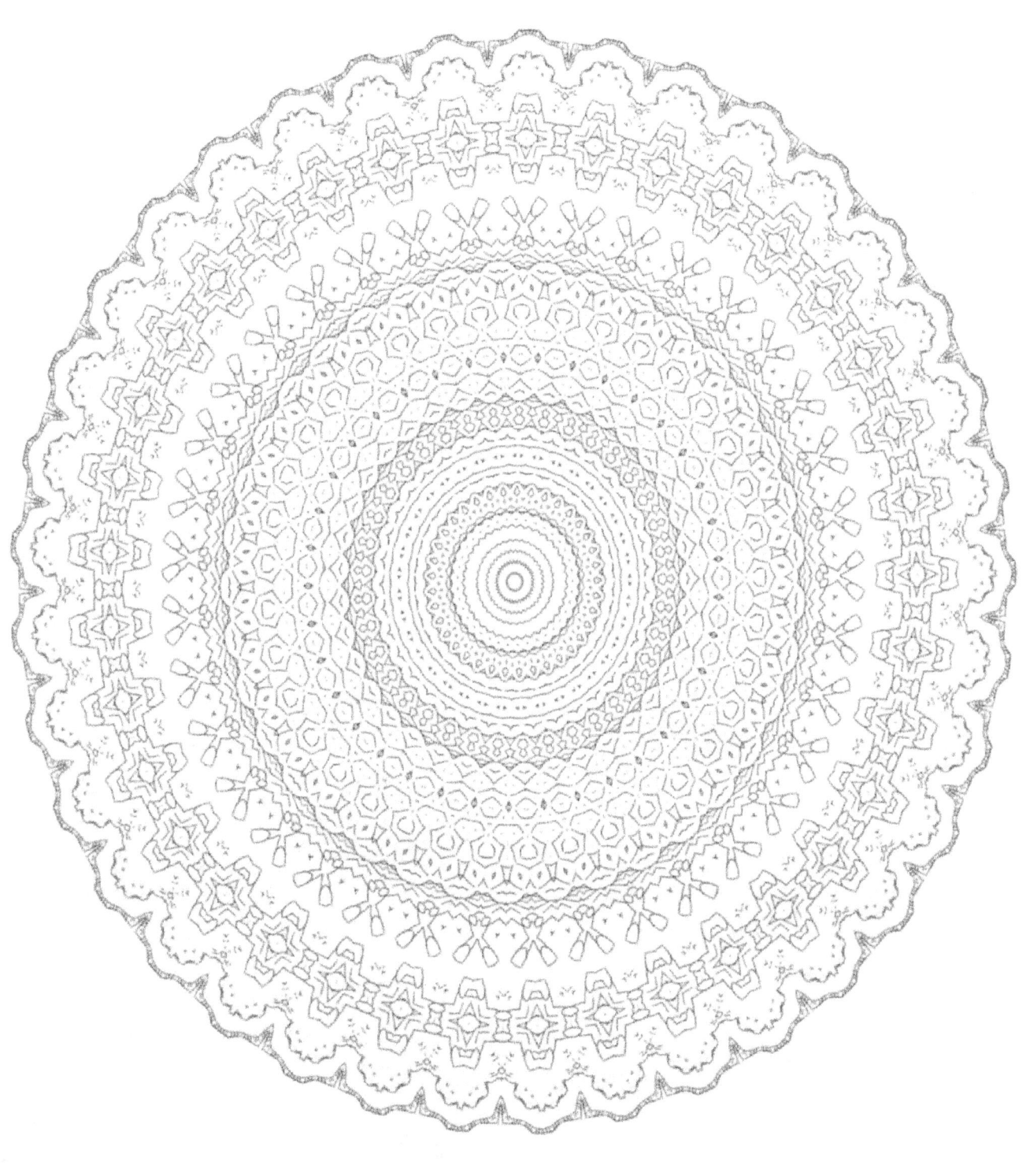

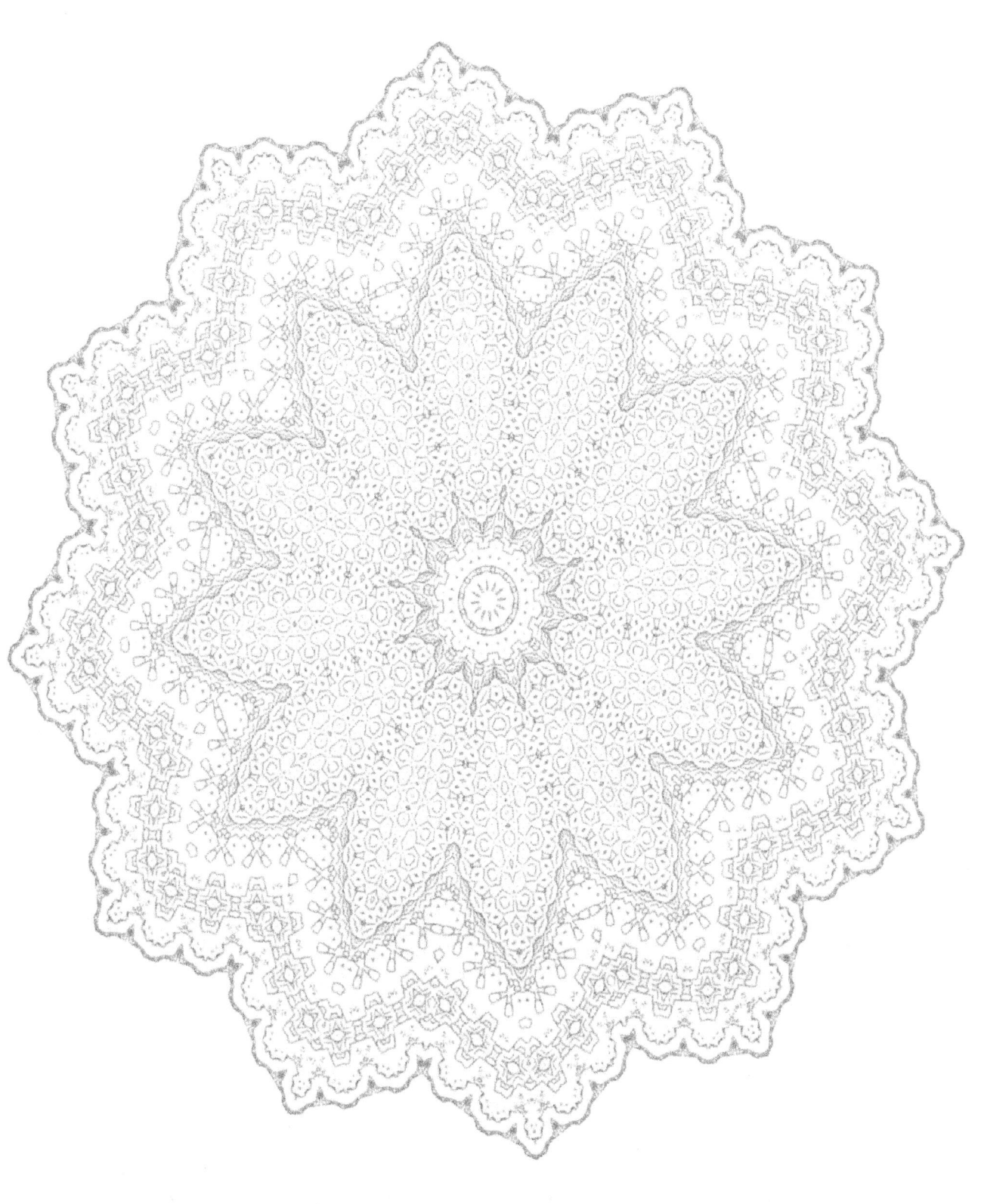

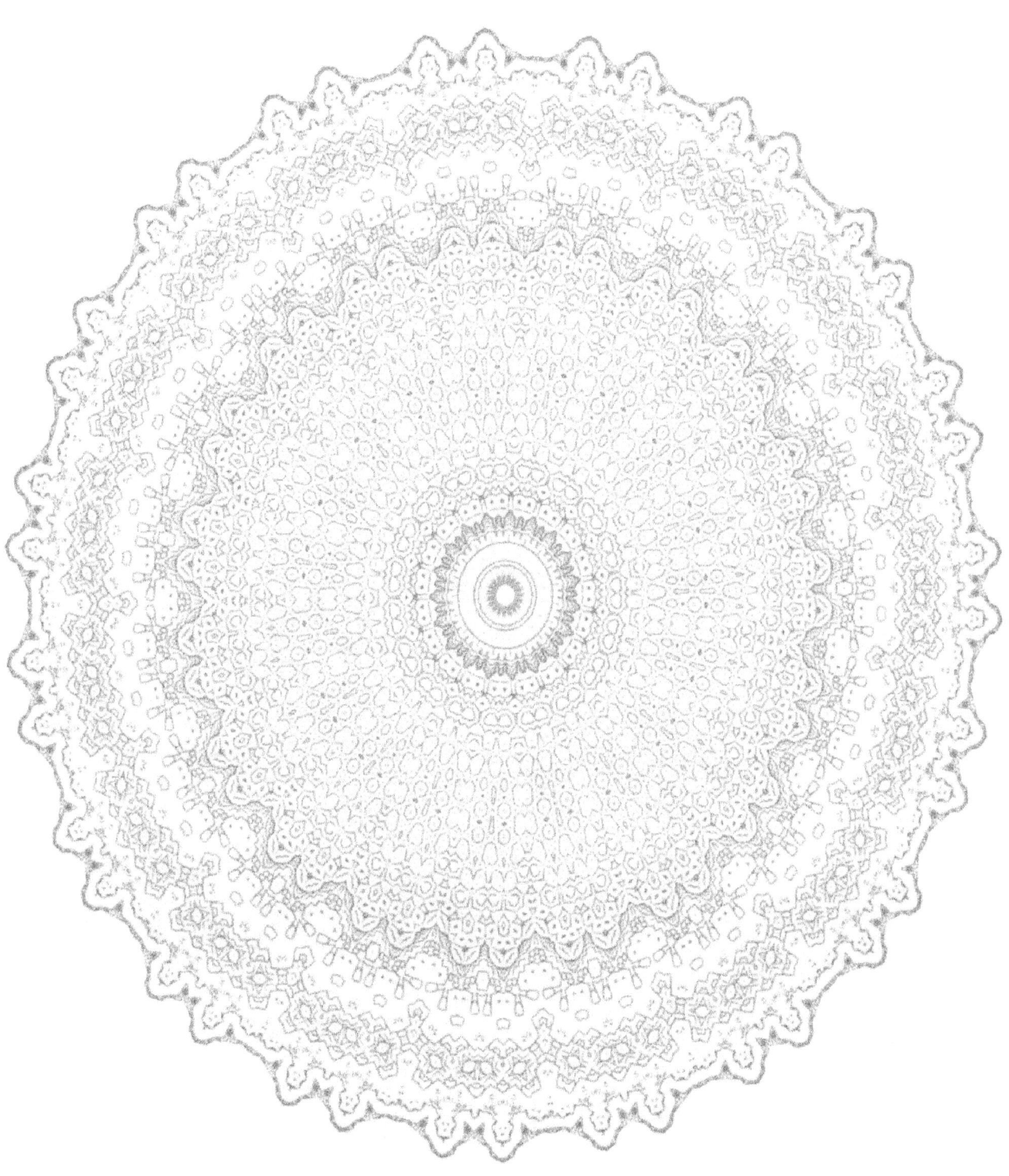

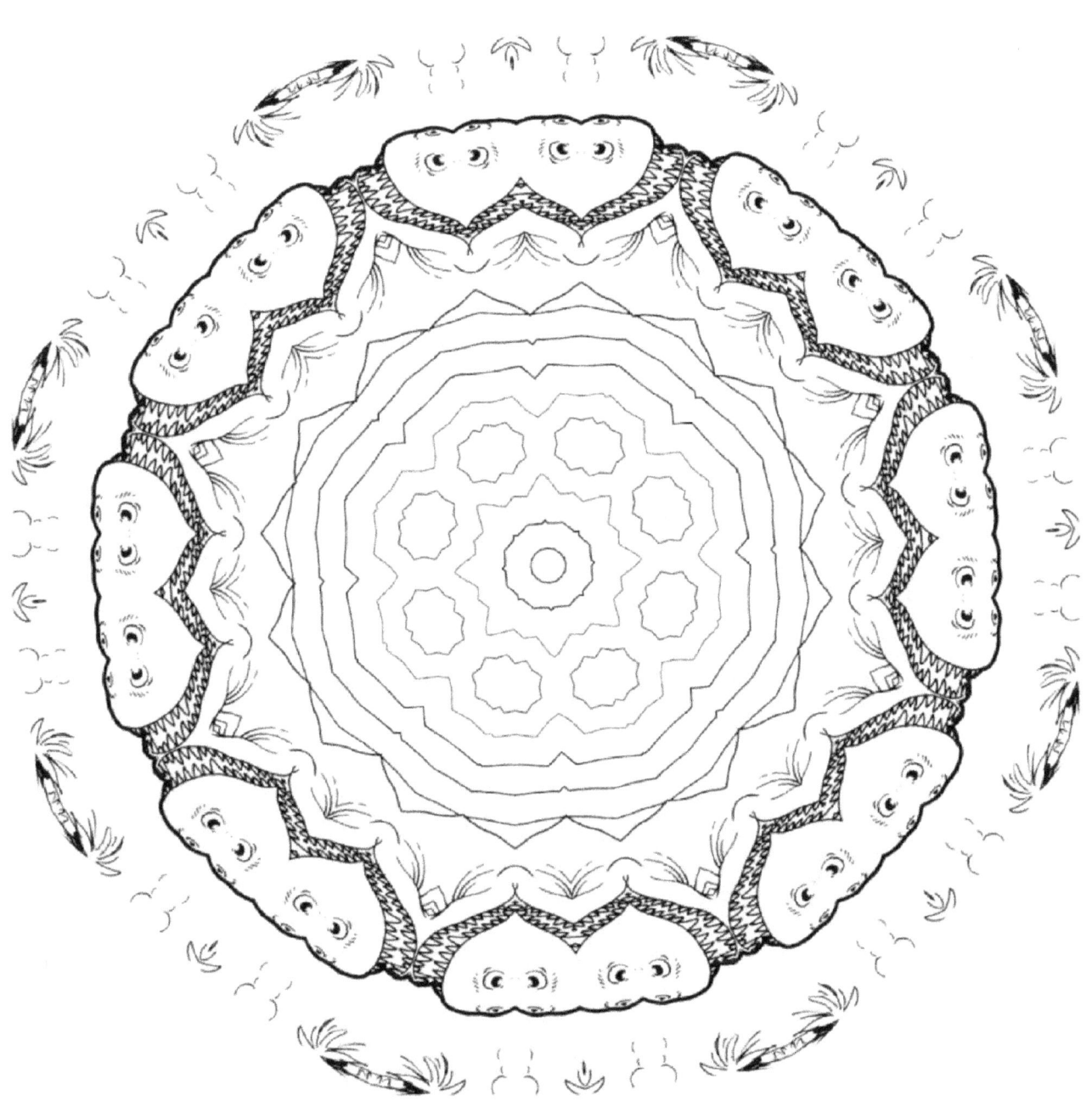

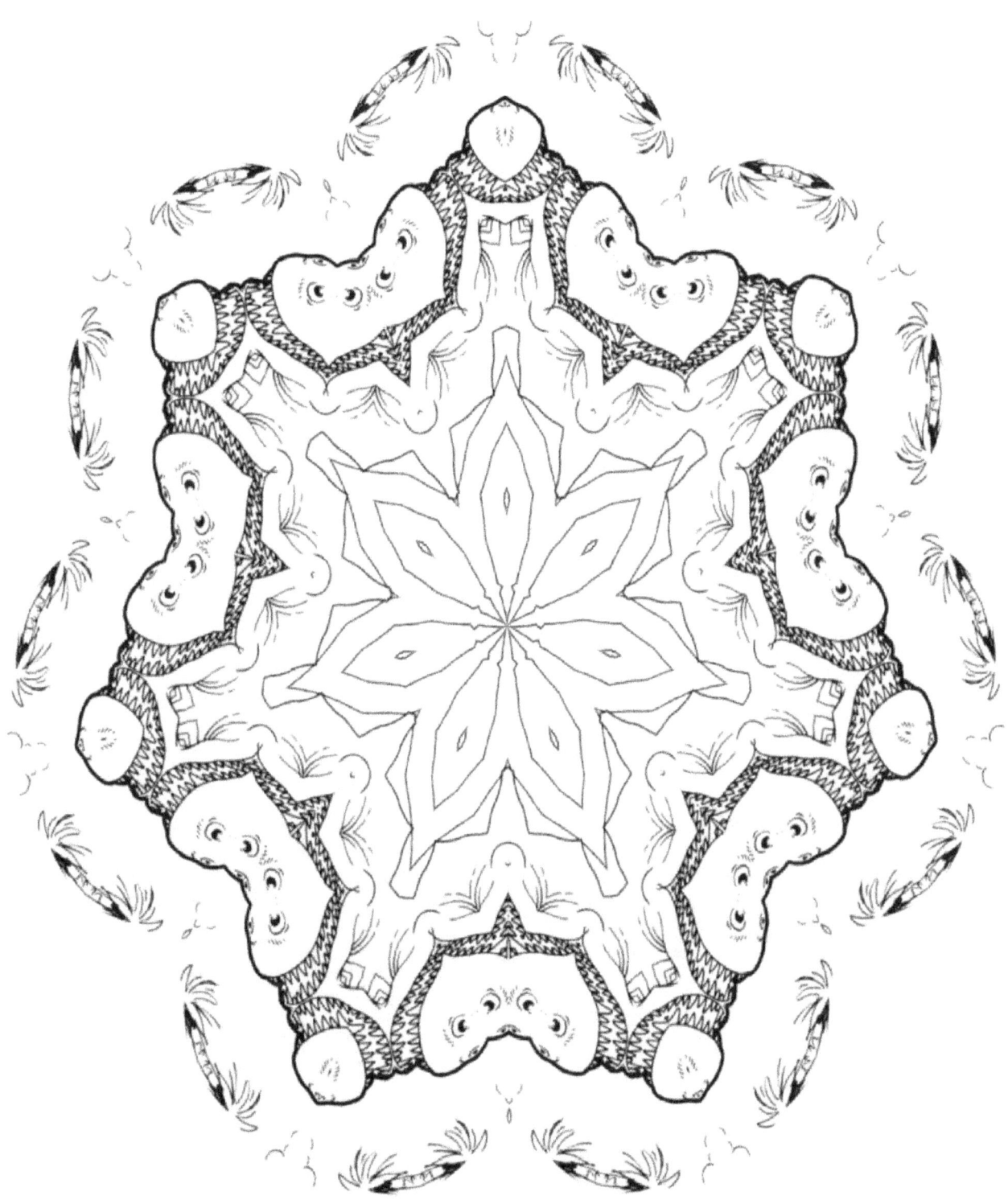

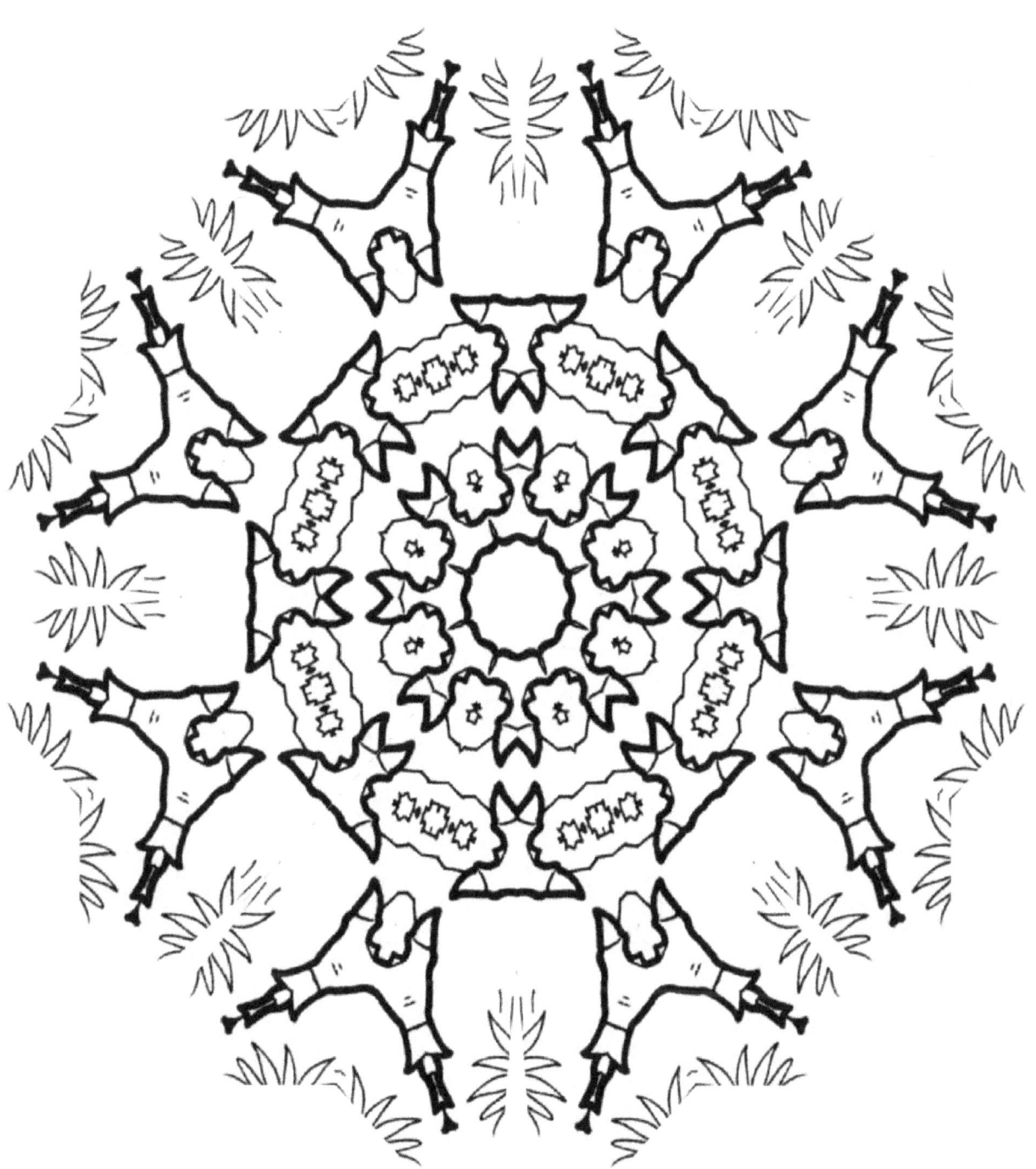

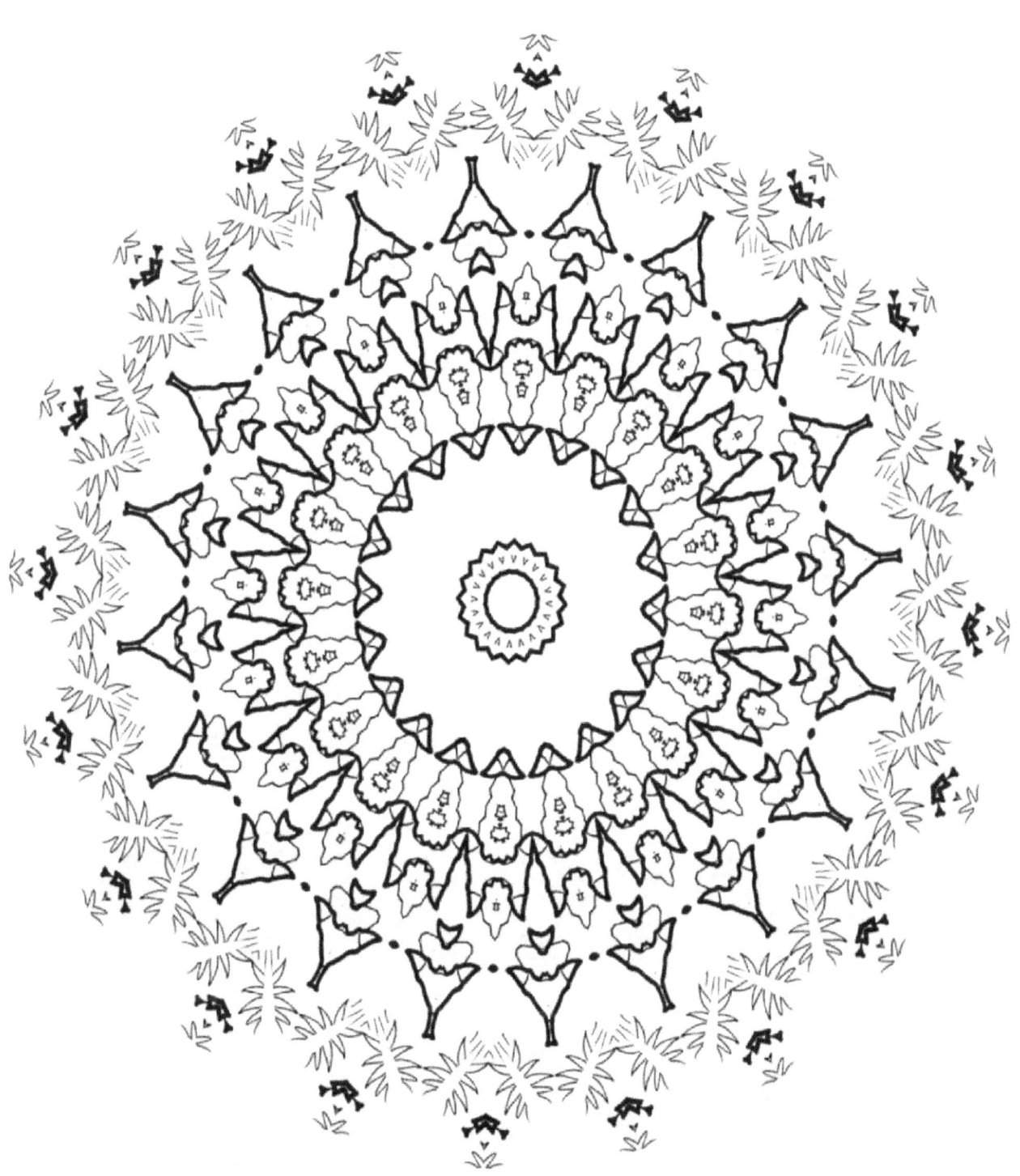

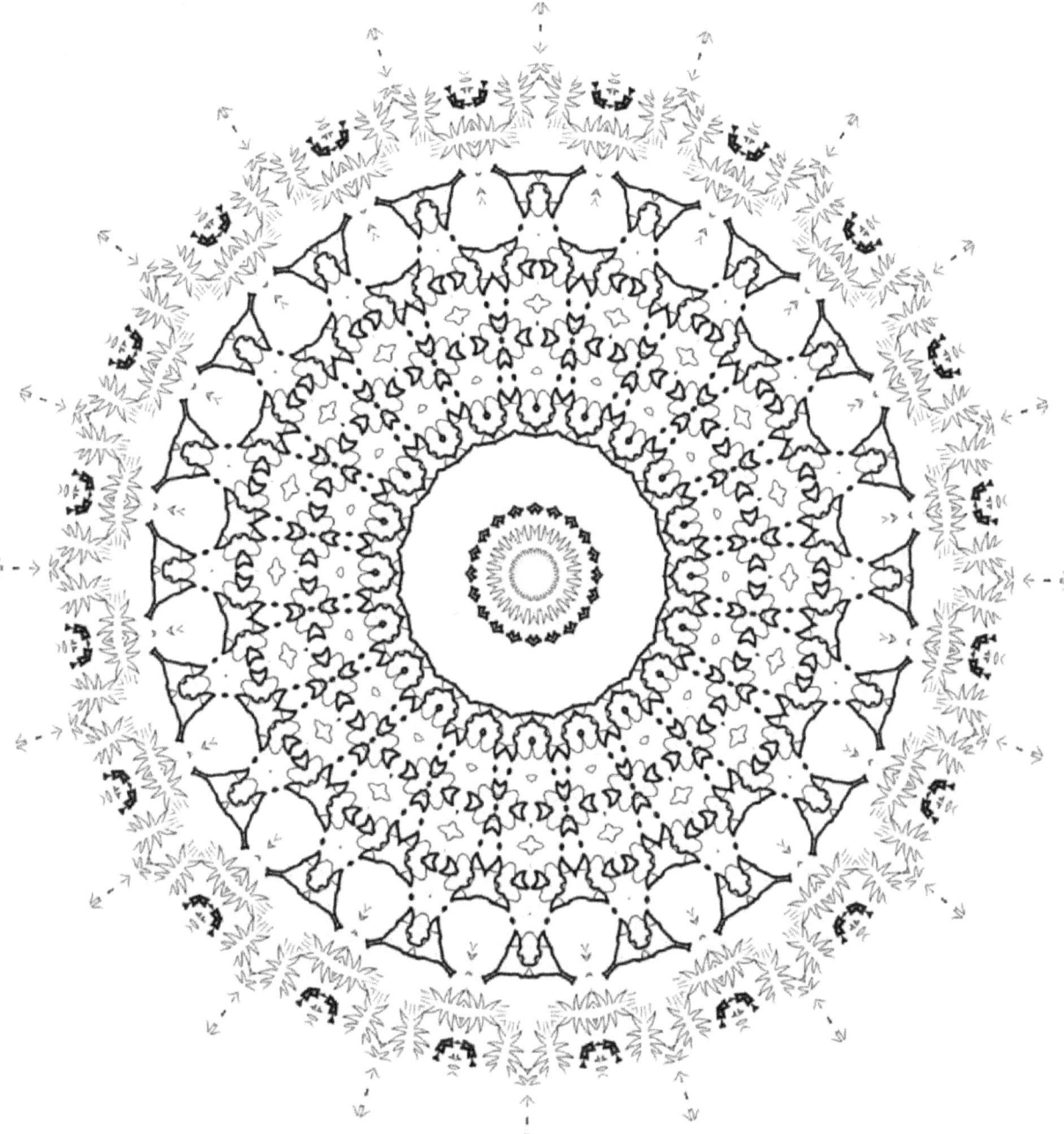

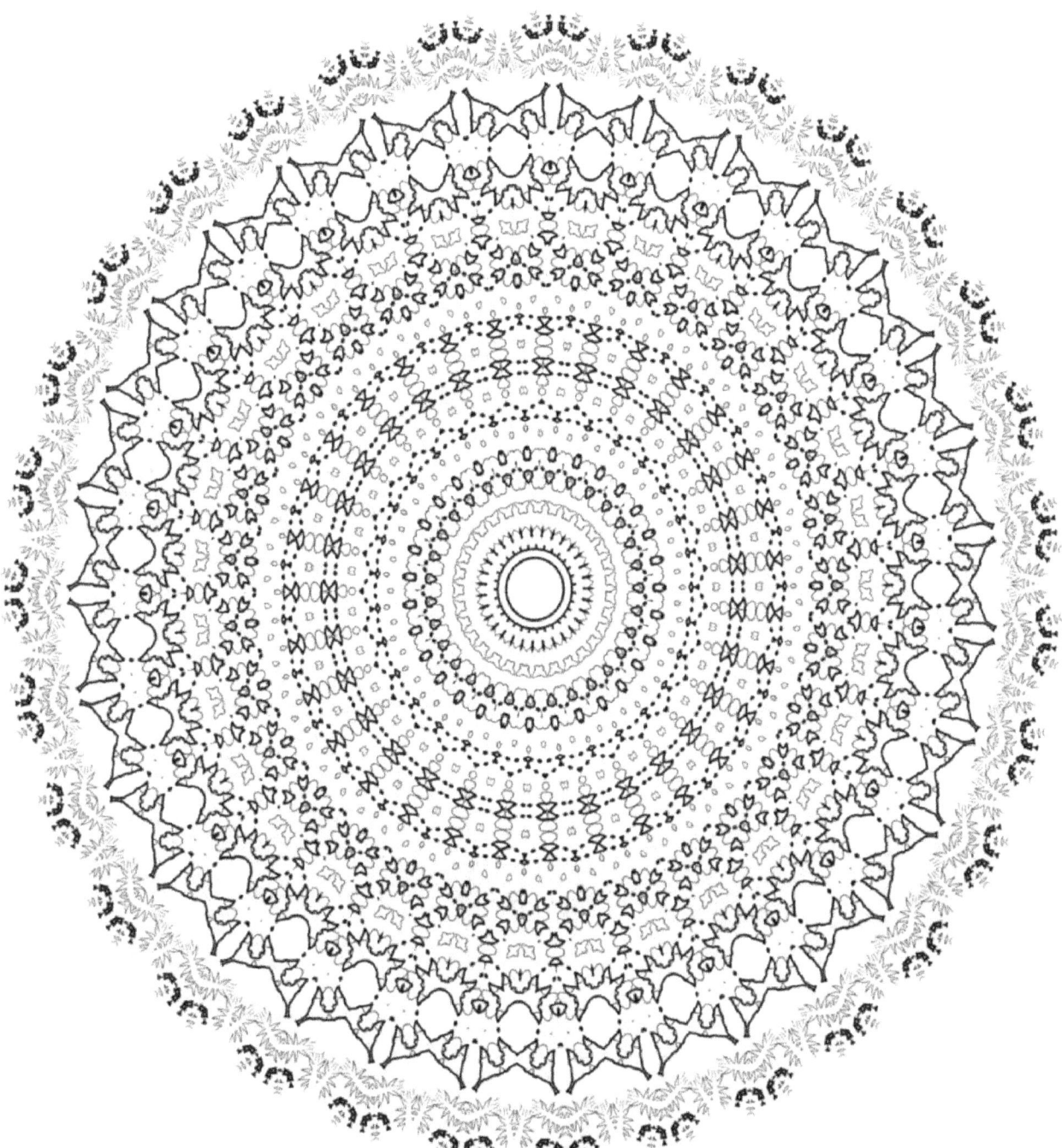

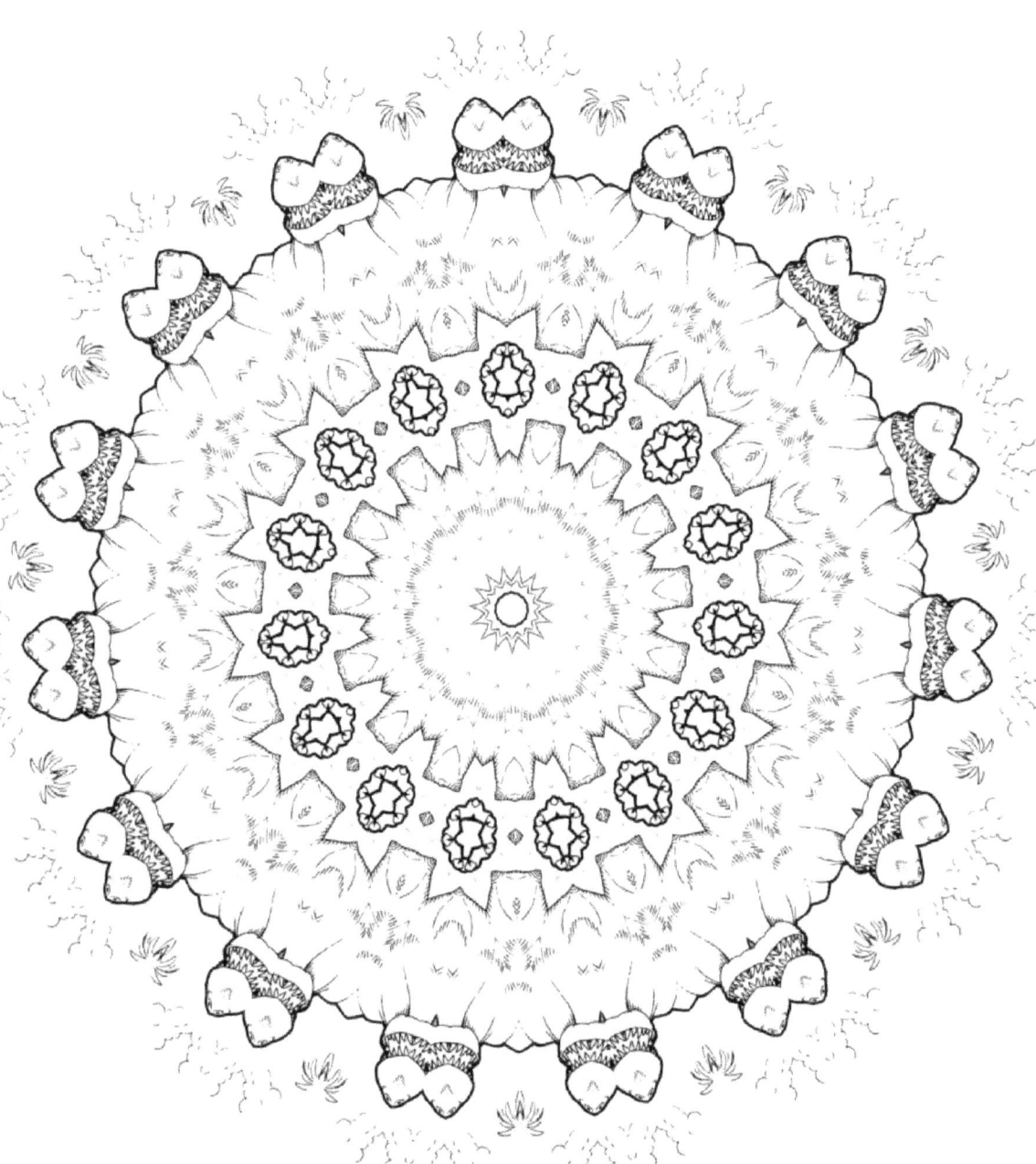

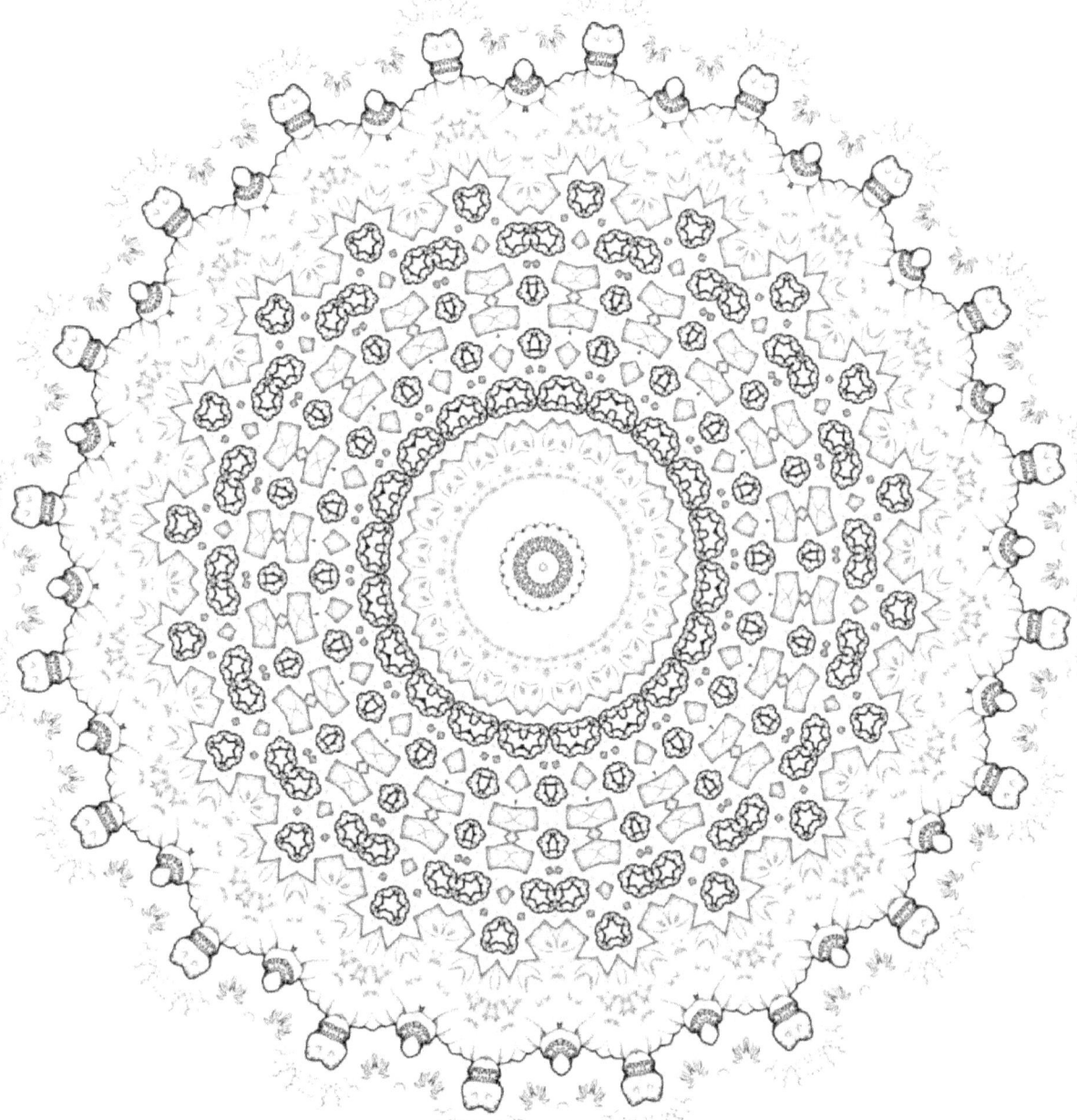

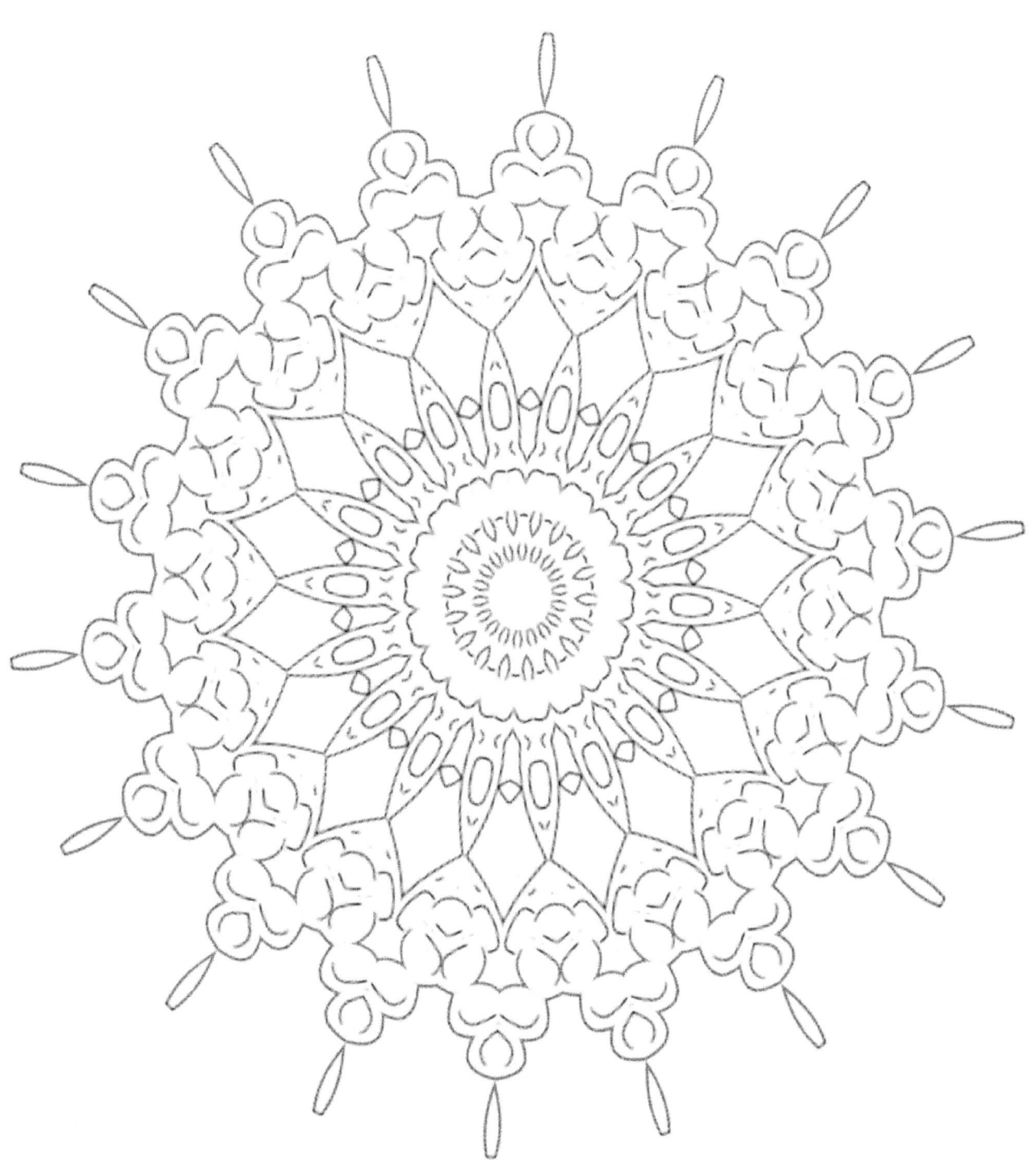

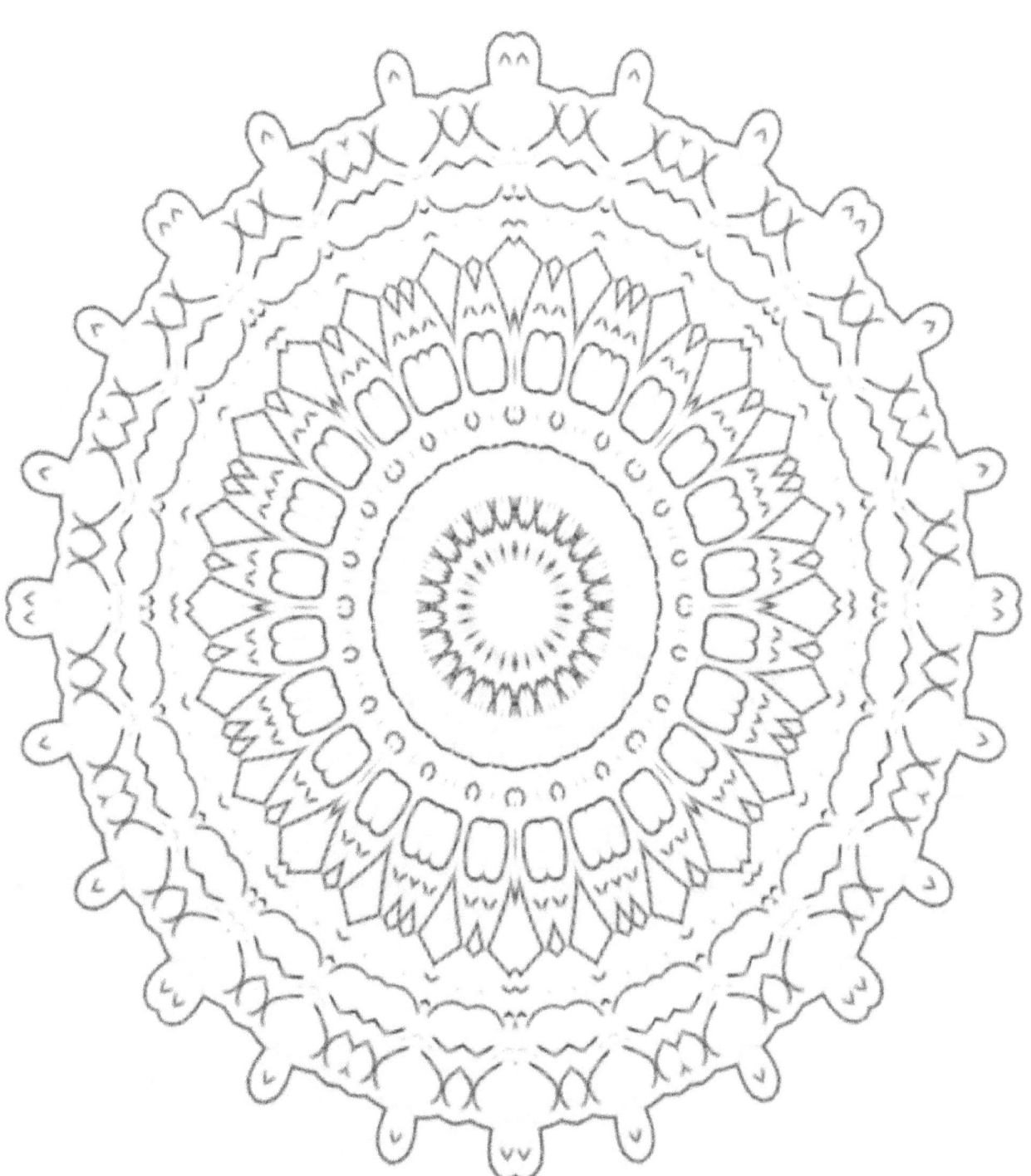

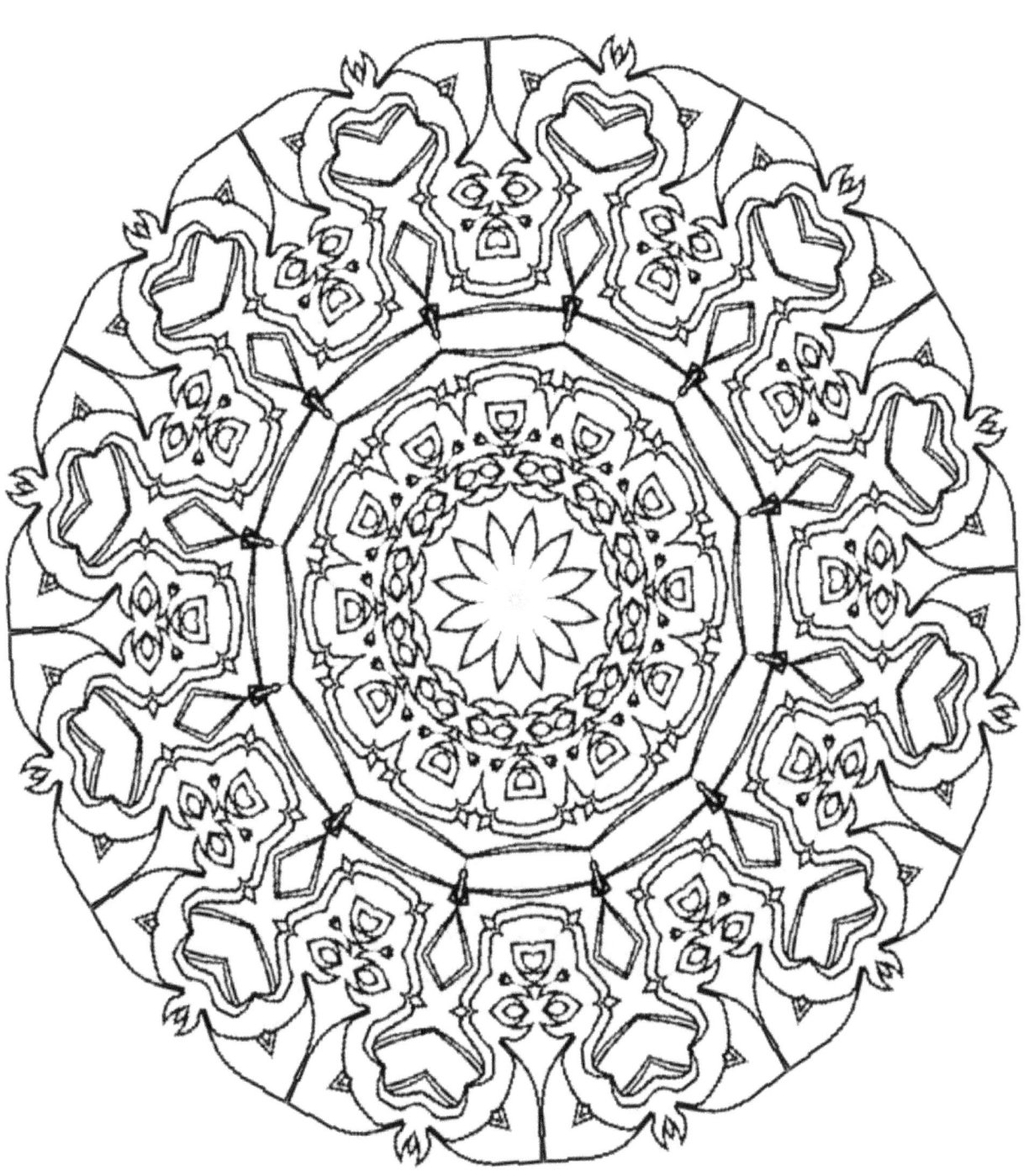

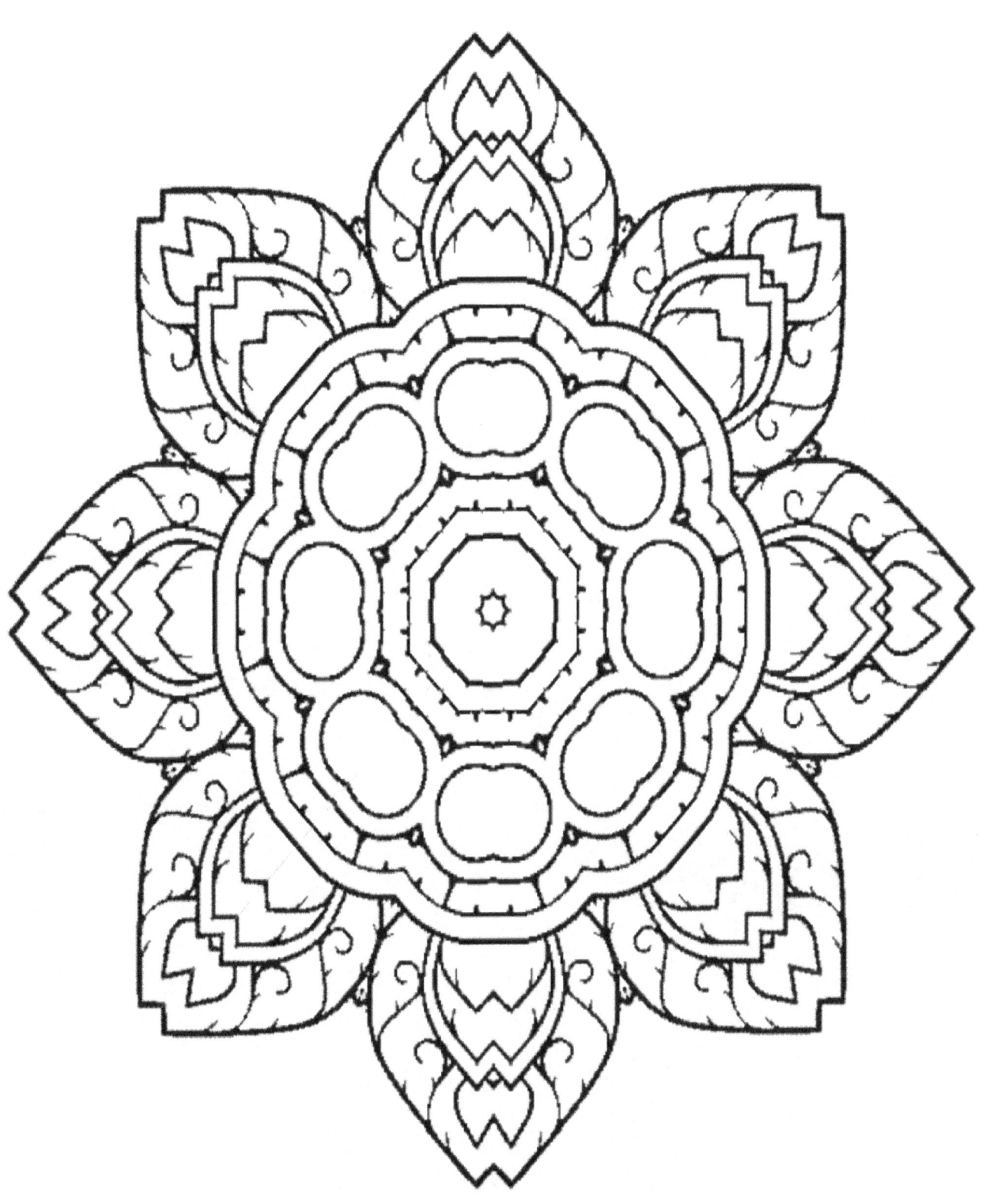

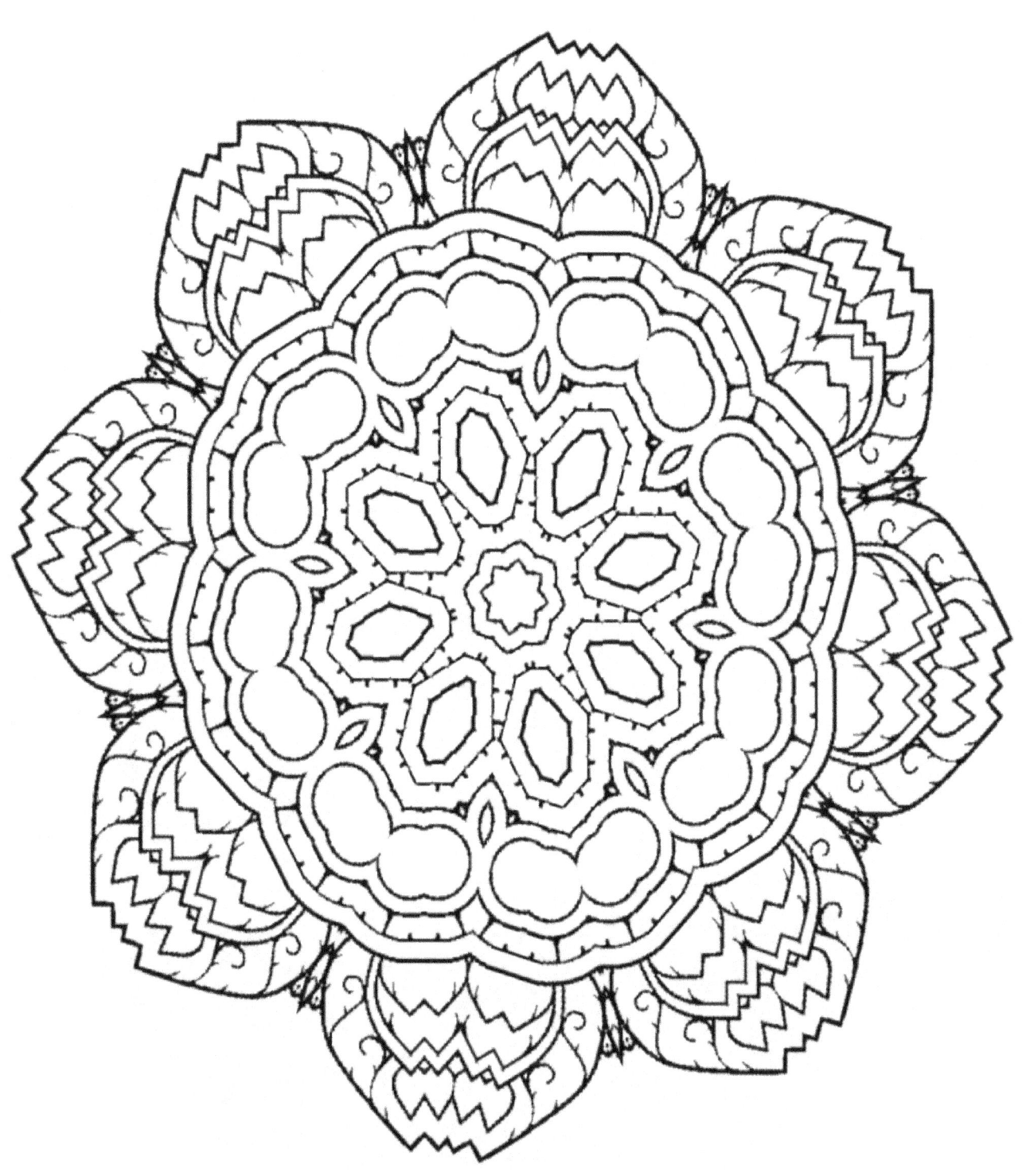

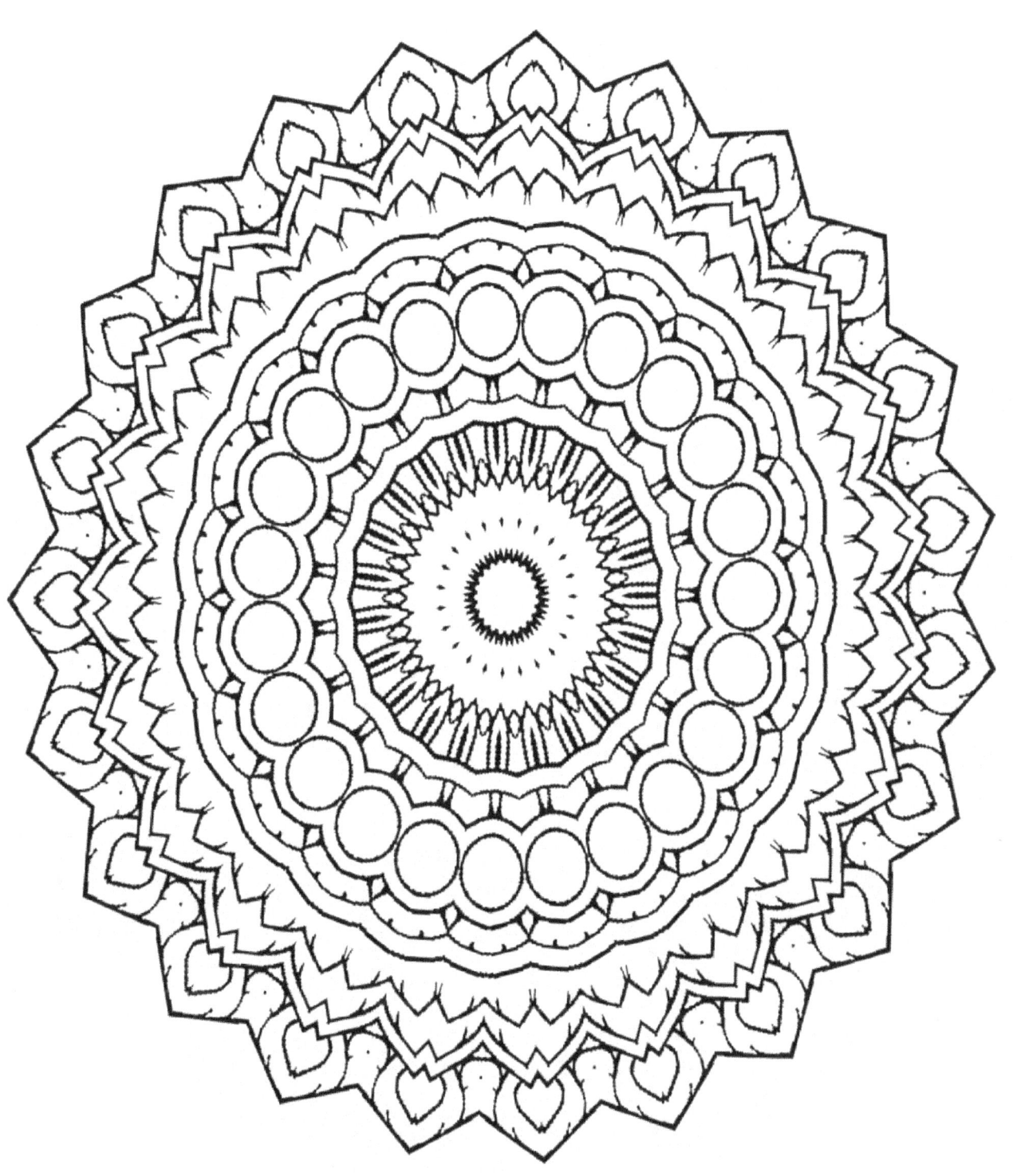